JON DAVIDSON

OF BOMBS AND BLACKBERRIES

JON DAVIDSON

THE ONLY GUIDE TO LIFE YOU WILL EVER NEED

Printed in the United States of America
First Printing, 2012

Safe Silver Press
1921 SE 176th Ave
Portland, OR 97233-4738

Safe Silver Press is an imprint and DBA of Crown Point Entertainment, LLC

Cover design: James Fletcher and TheLabDesign
Interior design: Jon Davidson
Back Cover Photo: Russell Stafford

www.jondavidsonmusic.com
www.jondavidsonmusic.blogspot.com

A percentage of the proceeds from the sale of this book will be donated to Tucker-Maxon Oral School, an incredible institution for hearing-impaired children in Portland, OR. For more information on Tucker-Maxon, visit www.tmos.org.

ISBN-13:
978-0615601106 (Safe Silver Press)

ISBN-10:
0615601103

Library of Congress Control Number: 2012902757

DEDICATION.

This book is dedicated to my parents, Dr. Richard and Dr. Jo Ann Davidson. Yes, they get mail addressed to Dr. and Dr. Davidson. They've authored some 10 books between them, and they instilled in me a love for the literary arts from a young age, in addition to being the greatest parents a guy (or girl, or anything in between) could ask for. Plus, they are solely responsible for my great genes. I'm proud to be joining the ranks of Davidson writers with this feeble attempt at authorship. Mom, don't think for a second that I love you any less just because Dad has a chapter in this book and you don't. I'm saving yours for my next volume. Love you both lots!

CONTENTS.

ACKNOWLEDGMENTS.

I would like to thank God for his grace and twisted sense of humor. I'd also like to thank my friends and fans who have been involved with many of the experiences recounted in this volume. Thanks to the members of Crown Point and Silversafe for putting up with my unbelievable talent and my humility. Thanks to my mom and dad for your indomitable faith in me and my musical and literary career. Thanks to Mandy Krohn for being my primary sounding board. Thanks to Jay and Nancy Crawford, Cheryl Airy, Chuck Gray, Kim Johnson, Eric and Cindy Rimkeit, and so many more for your generosity. Thanks to James Fletcher for simply being the greatest graphic designer on the face of the planet. Thanks to Minisaurus for keeping my lap and, alternatingly, my legs warm during the writing of this book.

Thanks to the sextet of authors who have inspired me as of late: A.J. Jacobs, Bill McKibben, Joel Heng Hartse, Donald Miller, Rick Reilly, and John Ortberg.

I would also like to thank my tireless editorial staff, consisting solely of myself. I am forever indebted.

Thanks to you for buying, borrowing, stealing, gaffling, or otherwise procuring this book. I'm not concerned with how you got your grubby little hands, or your well-manicured midsize hands, on it. I *would* thank you for reading it, as well, but you've barely gotten through the acknowledgements, and this is not an accomplishment worthy of my gratitude. I'll make sure to say thanks at the end.

INTRODUCTION.

If you've had the distinct privilege of spending any amount of time with me, you know by now that I'm an opinionated guy. What's more, you've realized that I often present my opinions as fact. What better way to cement these opinions as such than to remove them from the malleable medium of a blog and print them indelibly in this volume?

If you read it in a book, you know it's true.

It is my intent that this book reads as a collection of short stories. *Creative (non)fiction,* as the Library Of Congress might call it. As a result, you'll find references to events in the past interspersed with rants and tangents (rantgents?) about things that I currently hate, or at least somewhat convincingly pretend to hate. You might even find a few chapters about things I *don't* hate. I have adapted a couple of the chapters in this book from my blog, Rhetorock, which you can and will follow at jondavidsonmusic.blogspot.com. However, I've removed any sense of chronological order.

My mind rarely sits still. Metaphorically. Physically, it's typically firmly lodged inside my skull. Right now, I'm simultaneously thinking about bath salts, kidney beans, Levi's 510s, Jeremiah, Obamacare, Keane, and why I put my underwear on inside out again. Rather than attempt to tame the meandering beast that is my stream of consciousness, I've written in a way that reflects my usual thought processes. You're welcome.

Opinions represented in this book are solely mine, although I suppose that probably goes without saying. Some opinions have changed since I've written certain chapters. I've completely fabricated some opinions for the sake of discussion and entertainment, and to try to make others look stupid. However, some of the opinions I've expressed are completely serious. Feel free to disagree with me on anything and everything. Use your judgment, and take everything I've penned with a grain of salt. Better yet, with a massive salt lick. Make sure it's iodized salt, though. Goiters are really not all that cool.

If you're offended by anything that I've written, I sincerely apologize. You have taken me way too seriously. Write me an angry letter, and then take that letter and light it on fire.

It is my hope that this book makes you laugh, cry, and ponder. Simultaneously, you big thoughtful blubbering mess.

Life is short, and we're not given a lot of time on this earth. I hope you enjoy the time you spend with this book.

STOP TALKING. START DOING.

Ah, the dichotomy that is Thanksgiving.

On the one hand, it's the only national holiday, in my opinion, that has retained much of its original, beautiful meaning and purpose, which is, of course, slaughtering turkeys, celebrating obesity, and taking land from indigenous people.

In all seriousness, it's great that we have a day set aside for the sole purpose of giving thanks for the good things in our lives. However, if you work retail, you really don't have a lot to be thankful for this time of year. And, if you're Canadian, you celebrate a different date altogether in your tireless yet fruitless attempt to be viewed as more than just America's oddly shaped hat.

On the other hand, though, all the warm, fuzzy altruism of Thanksgiving Thursday is quickly swallowed up by the rampant consumerism that is Black Friday. These days, the clock doesn't even get to peacefully strike 10 PM on Thanksgiving before major sales begin at numerous nationwide retailers, including Walmart.

Thankfully, no one was trampled to death in this last year's savings scrum. Instead, we saw consumers handling the shopping stress in much more mature, considerate ways: with knives, guns and pepper spray.

God bless America.

I realize that countless individuals have already come to these same conclusions; I'm not breaking any ideological new ground here. However, never has this inherent dichotomy been more apparent to me than on this last Thanksgiving Day.

I, like most Americans, spent my Thanksgiving Day awash in self-indulgent gluttony. By three PM, I'd already gorged myself, and a happy little food fetus was growing inside of me. (I will withhold the details of the birth of said child.) I watched two and a half NFL games. I think I got up off the couch a grand total of four times in eight hours.

At nine PM, I was craving orange juice. Trop50, to be exact. Sweetened with stevia. Less sugar. All natural. Cures mumps.

Who has the largest selection of orange juice in America? Walmart, that's who. Walmart even carries blood orange juice, which, of course, is orange juice squeezed in a war zone and used to finance an insurgency. So, forgetting all the ads I'd seen throughout the day about the Thursday Black Friday sale kickoff, I drove to the typically unassuming Walmart Supercenter on Mill Plain in Vancouver, WA.

Yes, you hate on Walmart because it's trendy to do so. And yes, you still shop there anyway.

Upon arrival, the fact that there was a parking lot attendant directing traffic should have been my first clue. Upon entering, I was greeted by the sight of literally over a thousand people milling around the store like frugal, questionably sentient zombies, some pushing multiple carts, all waiting for the clock to strike ten so that they could save $6 on their video games or buy another ridiculously cheap, soon-to-be-obsolete 3D TV, thereby ensuring that their family wouldn't have to interact at all for at least another year.

At least these zombies weren't jacked on bath salts and eating face. Every cloud has a silver lining.

Pushing my way through hordes of the undead who were gathered around a guy who was break dancing in the frozen foods aisle (seriously), and through another group clustered around two hopelessly overweight women blubbering rotund threats at each other, I grabbed my Trop50.

I also needed to purchase shampoo, conditioner, and body wash. I hit the jackpot: Suave 3 in 1. It's all three of the aforementioned products, all in one inexpensive milky blue fluid. It also moonlights as antifreeze and a baby food. And, it smells great.

I have learned the hard way that most bath and hygiene products, this one included, smell a lot better than they taste. Trust me on this one.

I paid and left.

However, I couldn't shake the sickened feeling in my stomach. Hundreds of thousands of families across America, spending what little potential quality time they had with each other waiting in line to buy the next thing they didn't need.

I stopped for gas on the way home, at a Texaco that I never go to because it's never all that cheap. But, it was the only station open, so I pulled in and was greeted by a smiling little old lady. Never once complaining about the cold weather or the fact that she was working, alone, on Thanksgiving, she pumped my gas, washed my windshield, and asked me all about how my holiday had been.

As she was washing my rear window, I reached into my wallet and took out a $5.

When she handed me my receipt, I handed her the Lincoln. She looked at me strangely and reminded me that I'd already paid with my credit card.

"That's for you," I said. "Thanks for smiling. Happy Thanksgiving." "That's too much," she said. I insisted that she take it, suddenly feeling the weight of my own selfishness.

Her eyes filled with tears. "Thank you," she said. "No, thank *you*," I said, and drove off.

As soon as I pulled out of the station and onto Stark Street, I burst into tears, my mind a mess.

Jesus had it right. It is so much better to give than to receive.

What if? What if I had spent my Thanksgiving at a homeless shelter or a soup kitchen? What if I would've given that lady a $20 instead of thinking about how much I needed the money? What if I had taken the time to call or text some people and let them know how thankful I am for them? What if I would've done anything besides stuff my face and rot my brain on this, the appointed day for giving thanks? And, more importantly, why do I need a federal holiday to remind me to be, for three minutes at a deserted gas station, the kind of person that I want to be 24/7?

One simple act of giving so little was the best thing that happened to me all day.

Maybe I need to figure a few things out. Stop talking. Start doing.

BOBBLE BABBLE.

Nowadays, everyone has their own bobblehead doll.

Pope Benedict XVI has one. So does each member of the cast of Jersey Shore. A few years from now, The Situation's bobblehead will likely become the first doll to die of skin cancer.

I recently went to a Seattle Mariners game where the first 20,000 fans were given free Ichiro bobbleheads. Sadly, bobbleheads are now so ubiquitous and the Mariners are so awful that even this promotion couldn't put 20,000 people in the seats to watch their moribund home team self-destruct and lose another game.

I'm a White Sox fan, for the record. 2005, baby. No silly compasses in our logo. Plus, our bobbleheads are of truly upstanding players, like Shoeless Joe Jackson.

Fortunately, bobbleheads weren't as popular during Major League Baseball's infamous steroid era. Manufacturers would have had to find a way to make the heads of Mark McGwire or Barry Bonds bobbles increase dramatically in size over the course of ten years or so.

The Roger Clemens bobblehead, if made to scale, would actually have the biggest, jowliest head of any bobblehead known to man. Talk about a serious jowl movement. The makers would probably have to make the Clemens bobble constantly appear sweaty and deceitful, as well.

Not feelin' America's pastime? (Note the conspicuous absence of the word 'sport' here.) No problem. Plenty of other notable figures have gotten in on the bobblehead action.

Mel Gibson. The Beatles. Barack Obama. Darth Vader.

Jesus. Available with or without the crown of thorns. Seriously.

They even made a Marie Antoinette bobblehead, but were forced to recall the entire run because the head wouldn't stay on.

Too soon?

You can custom-order a bobblehead in your likeness for only $79 from custombobbleheads.com, if you want to leave a legacy.

One thing that I really like about bobbleheads is that they're so agreeable. Have you ever seen a bobblehead shake its head no? In other words, ladies, they make the ideal boyfriend.

Kinda makes me want to design a naysaying bobblehead and send it to a few people, without further explanation. Chris Berman, Glenn Beck, Miley Cyrus, Newt Gingrich, and Sarah Palin, in no particular order, come to mind. The dissentient bobbleheads would, of course, be in their respective likenesses, so their recipients would initially be flattered, only to be later overcome with disappointment as a toy caricature of themselves shook its head in constant general disapproval.

I'm beginning to realize how little I actually know about bobbleheads. I don't even know where they came from. However, I do know where to find the answer.

Naturally, when confronted with a need for cold, hard facts, I turn to that irrefutable, immutable source, Wikipedia.

Apparently, bobbleheads originated in ancient Mesopotamia. According to Scripture, sinful people attempted to build a tower to heaven, a tower with a giant, mobile head. They called it the Tower Of Bobble. God, displeased with their lack of faith, and with their lack of foresight for not having put the likeness of his head on the tower, struck the skyscraper with lightning, shattering it into a million little bobbleheads.

What's that? You're not buying it? Obviously you're not reading the right verses. Turn to the book of Genesis—it's the first book of the Holy Bobble.

As you might have guessed, I'm writing at 3 AM again.

In all seriousness, bobbleheads rose to popularity in the 1950s, but they were invented long before that. Proto-bobbleheads were first mentioned in a short story by some Russian novelist named Gogol in 1842. I've never heard of him, so clearly he does not matter.

I tried to Google Gogol (say that five times fast), and the band Gogol Bordello came up. I am a quasi-fan, although I had forgotten that they existed until the aforementioned Gogol Googling. It turns out that they took the first part of their name from this author guy. Hooray.

Hopefully, this is the most useless fact that you will come across in the course of reading this book. If not, I'll give you your money back, but unfortunately I can't refund the time you've wasted.

I'm sorry.

In this case, the only appropriate action for you to take would be to send me one of those disapproving Jon Davidson bobblehead dolls.

CAULIFLOWER. SATAN'S PLANTAR WART.

In this era of exponential proliferation of digital media, one sense has gone the way of the Walkman.

I'm talking, of course, about your sense of smell.

Of course, most people know by now that we have more than five senses. Yes, your mom lied to you. Again. Nociception, thermoception, and proprioception are all included on most scientific lists. (Yeah, I had to look those up.) Common sense, however, is conspicuously absent from lists these days.

That feeble joke was way too obvious. I apologize.

However, what's being done to our olfaction just plain stinks. Think about it: we digitally reproduce and transmit sights and sounds. Wii and Xbox controllers, of course, simulate movements and stimulate our sense of touch. Scientists at the 2011 UbiComp conference presented a method for digitally and electrically stimulating the tongue to produce taste sensations.

But smell? While companies such as AromaJet have devised cartridge-bearing smell-emitting devices to be paired with certain electronics, no one has figured out how to digitally reproduce scents. A Japanese company, however, says that it is currently working on a 3D TV equipped with digital touch and smell that will be available by 2020.

Impossible? Perhaps. I would imagine that the thought of digitally transmitting a video was deemed equally impossible by the scientific community not too long ago. "Preposterous, I say, Hiram! Now, return ye to draining some more blood from George Washington. We have only heretofore drained seven pints; perhaps when we remove his remaining three pints he shall recover."

Think about it, though. The applications of digital smell transmission are limitless! Smell a restaurant's food online before you visit. Test perfumes from the comfort of your home. Find out in advance if your Match.com date has dragon breath.

Who wouldn't want to text a fart to a friend?

Hopefully, Fear Factor, Red Lobster ads, NASCAR, and especially the burgeoning Scheisse porn industry wouldn't make use of this new technology.

Smell suffers from being one of the only senses that we can't easily mentally or manually override. You can close your eyes, wear earplugs or put in your iPod, remove your hand from the hot stove (why was it there in the first place, dummy?), or spit the cauliflower out of your mouth in order to stop receiving undesired sensory input.

By the way, cauliflower looks like one of Satan's plantar warts, tastes like one of Satan's plantar warts (trust me on this one), and should be eliminated from our society. Everyone who thinks they like cauliflower really only likes the ranch or cheese sauce that it's been dipped into.

To say that cauliflower smells like crap is an insult to crap itself.

It's hard to block your sense of smell. You can plug your nose, but this leaves you with the problem of not being able to breathe, since you also can smell the air breathed in through your mouth to a certain extent. This solution, in other words, will work for a couple minutes, but you are then presented with the unwelcome choice of either smelling some noxious odor for the second time, or else unconsciousness and imminent brain damage and death.

I guess that wearing a SARS mask would help somewhat. I've always wondered what the ramifications of simply wearing one of these around for a day would be, especially if the presence of the mask were accompanied by coughing, retching, foaming at the mouth, and a general pallor.

Perhaps, if the technology to digitally reproduce smell were available, the evil men and women in the world would, in a nefarious global scheme, begin bombarding the airwaves and our noses with the constant noxious stench of cooked cauliflower. Brave rebels with hearts of gold would fight the powers that be and inundate the air with the digital aroma of ranch dressing to counteract the cauliflower, until the world smelled like one giant picked-over veggie tray at the end of a crazy party.

So, Japan, maybe you should hold off on that new TV technology after all.

What is cauliflower's purpose on earth, anyway? And why do we have so many genetically altered cauliflower varieties? It's good to know that the brightest scientific minds of our day are finally putting their expertise to good use. Working on finding a cure for cancer is *so* 2002.

I would consider myself a demonstrative hater of cauliflower. I will not sit around and passively let this pale, ghastly scourge ruin me by finding its way into my mouth. I go out of my way to avoid dishes, restaurants, even whole continents who have anything to do with it. It's such a sneaky vegetable, too. What could possibly be accomplished by creating a faux mashed potato dish out of this masquerading miscreant of a vegetable? Last I checked, potatoes are full of nutrients and complex carbohydrates, and are the sole reason that Ireland is still a country and Idaho is even a state. Cauliflower is full of necrotic devil wart tissue.

Two quotes put the discrepancy between potato and cauliflower in perspective. Michael Pollan, the famous author, activist, and journalist, states: "Without the potato, the balance of European power might never have tilted north."[1] Satan, the famous demon, archfiend, and imp, states: "Cauliflower. Mmmm. Tastes like my warts and your souls."[2]

I rest my case.

GOUT IN LEFT FIELD.

Patience. Wish I could hurry up and find some.

I once wrote a song that included the lyric: "I pray for patience, and I need it right this second." Patience is a quality that I'm impatient for. Obviously, I need a South Beach Diet for the soul. 'Wait' and 'weight' are homophones, after all.

It almost seems as though patience is something genetic, something you're either born with or you're not. Like gout.

Actually, I'm not sure if gout is genetic. Since I'm writing this chapter on a flight to Chicago, I can't Google it without paying eleventeen dollars for in-flight wi-fi. I should've flown Delta. Guess I'll have to patiently wait till we land.

I always kind of wanted to get gout, just because I've always wanted to use the sentence "Sorry, my gout is flaring up again" in casual conversation during a fine dining experience. Or, "Pardon me, I'm having a bout with gout." In fact, if I were dictator of anything, I would dictate that all words containing 'out' should be upgraded to 'gout', simply for entertainment purposes.

Goutside Magazine. Goutlet mall. Goutdoor school. In-N-Gout Burger. Gout in left field. Down and gout. Goutback Steakhouse. Gouter space. The list is endless.

How does a Canadian pronounce "gout", anyway?

I digress. Thanks for patiently waiting for me to get back on track.

What makes some people casually let the person with fewer items behind them go ahead in the grocery line, while other people freak while an elderly lady attempts to find her checkbook? The foot tapping, the gum snapping, the exaggerated sighs. The curb stomps. The carnage.

It's funny how the speed of technology has completely changed our time paradigm. (Paratigm?) I remember growing up with my parents' slug-slow dialup internet connection, and actually having to set significant amounts of time aside to check my email. I also had to schedule time when no one else in our long-winded family needed to use the phone line.

Hulu? Every episode of South Park, free on Southparkstudios.com? Crown Point's hilarious YouTube videos (shameless plug)? Forget it.

On a side note, it's ironic that 'patience' and 'patients' are also homophones. When was the last time that you had an in-and-gout experience with a healthcare appointment? If you're more than 10 minutes late for your appointment, it gets canceled, yet the doctor can keep you waiting, seemingly capriciously, as long as he or she wants.

And, more importantly, why is it that the only magazine that hospitals subscribe to is *Cosmopolitan*? Thankfully, I have seized these waiting-room opportunities to learn all 50 secrets that will drive a man wild.

So what is patience, and where can I get some?

It seems that patience is more of a way of life than a spontaneous feeling. A deep-seated contentment that allows the individual who possesses it to be happy, despite, or perhaps because of, the ability to put their agendas and schedules on the back burner.

I often feel like patience and productivity can't go hand-in-hand. Truth is, though, it's the times when I'm the least stressed, the times when I am able to stop worrying about everything that I need to accomplish, that I'm able to be the most creative and the most productive.

I just put on my headphones. The guy beside me (truthfully, I thought he was a woman until he told me his name a few minutes ago) has had verbal diarrhea for the first hour of the flight, not to mention pepperoni-scented burps.

Ironically, I was impatient with the fact that he was impeding my progress on writing this chapter.

About patience.

Guess I have a lot to learn.

SIZE DOES MATTER.

Size does matter. Did I say that already?

When it comes to Alaska, everyone knows that everything is bigger.

Everything except for the cramped economy-class seat that I'm sitting in on my flight to Anchorage. Nothing but a flimsy armrest is keeping the kind lady seated next to me from oozing into my personal man-space.

However, Juneau that this is the last time I'll be cramped on this trip. Only a Homer doesn't Nome that Alaska is the biggest state in the US, and I'll have plenty of room to roam. Kenai tell you how excited I am to get there? My Haines are all in a wad, and I can't Barrow the suspense. If you don't think Alaska is unbelievable, you are in Denali. I'm looking forward to performing at the State Fair, where you can do everything from admire enormous pumpkins to watch professionals give a bear a body piercing or give a Yakutat. I might have to Wrangell for a place to Sitka at a few events, and hopefully I don't end up near anyone who smells like open Seward. I should probably stop at a store and Ketchikan of Axe Body Spray to take with me, just in case. I don't mean to beat a Deadhorse, but I Kiana can't wait to arrive.

That was quite possibly the cheesiest paragraph I've ever written. Somebody, please pry this laptop from my corny hands.

I seem to have digressed from what matters: Size. Length, width, girth: Alaska has it all. One would assume that significant shrinkage would occur due to the cold, but Alaska has managed to retain its original dimensions.

I once saw a t-shirt with the outline of Alaska encompassing the outline of Texas, with the caption "Ain't Texas Cute?"

Did you know that the land area of the city limits and borough of Juneau, Alaska's capital city, is larger than Rhode Island and Delaware *combined*? And that Juneau is only Alaska's third-largest city by area?

You could fit over five Oregons, or 425 Rhode Islands, neatly inside Alaska's boundaries.

Sorry, Texas. You got pwned.

Alaska's state flag was designed by 13-year-old Bennie Benson. Really creative work, dummypants. You just added a stray star to the Big Dipper.

Alaska is the northernmost, westernmost, and easternmost state in the United States, thanks to the 180° meridian. Look it up, and impress your friends.

Alaska's state sport is dog mushing, using time-tested recipes for such favorites as Schnauzer Stew and Great Dane Gruel.

Alaska's name, of course, is derived from an old Aleutian word, which means "Give Us Back Our Land And Oil, Stupid White Man."

Russell, my bandmate in Crown Point, a grown man of sound mind, literally just learned about four hours ago that the plural of "moose" was, in fact, not "meese". This is a true story.

Unfortunately, what you might have read, or, more likely, seen in the *Simpsons Movie* about the Alaska state government paying individuals to move to The Last Frontier simply *isn't* true. I checked. However, since 1976, qualifying permanent residents of Alaska have been receiving dividends from The Permanent Fund, which essentially reinvests oil and gas revenues. The good news is that the state government pays quite well. The bad news is that they pay exclusively in whale blubber.

Through a break in the clouds, I can see massive Mt. Fairweather. Our bubbly flight attendant has just informed us that "it's that magic hour where we get to put away our electronic devices." What are we, twelve? "Jonny, have we cleaned our room?" "Mom, if this is a team effort, you certainly haven't done your part." And magic hour? Really, lady? Does my laptop turn into a rabbit when I put it in the case?

I know better than to argue with flight attendants, though. I'm reminded of the famous story of Muhammad Ali's refusal to buckle up on a flight in the late 1960s. "Superman don't need no seatbelt," Ali told a flight attendant. "Superman don't need no airplane," she retorted.

Despite my burgeoning ego, I doubt you'll ever catch me referring to myself in the third person superhero tense.

How many athletes, enormously successful though they may be, are going to claim "Superman" as their moniker, anyway? If I were forced to pick an ostentatious nickname, I'd go the Randy Johnson route. You can't disrespect the "Big Unit."

Alaska should seriously consider changing *its* nickname, too. The Last Frontier sounds rustic and bucolic. The Big Unit sounds, well, Casanova. Too bad Mrs. Palin isn't running the joint anymore. I bet she'd be all over that.

THAT INKY GREEK DARKNESS.

I can't even begin to express my disappointment.

Apparently, the coolest irregular plural noun of all time is no more.

Octopi? Out. Octopuses? In.

This precipitous fall from plural grace is comparable, in my opinion, to glasnost and the fall of Communism in Russia. While Russia did have to lose the Soviet Union moniker, it at least didn't have to suffer from the emasculating embarrassment of its name now ending in 'puses.'

Russiapus is pretty fun to say, though.

Unbeknownst to me, 'octopuses' has been the correct plural form all along. Seems that the word 'octopus' has a Greek etymology, and therefore the correct plural suffix is –es, not –i. This is dumb. 'Octopi' sounds awesome.

Some literary sources prefer the use of the plural term 'octopodes.' This is derived from the name of the animal's taxonomic order, *Octopoda. Fowler's Modern English Usage* calls this form pedantic. If you say 'octopodes,' you probably wear a pocket protector, and think that the 'game' referred to when talking about having game with the ladies is, in fact, chess. So, shut up. Your pretentious plural form is officially out of the discussion.

I grew up using ‘octopi.’ Not using the animal, typically, but rather using the word. It’s shorter, sounds better, and makes me think of an octo-pie. Eight pies in one. Coconut cream, key lime, apple, marionberry. Get in my mouth.

Octomom, on the other hand, can stay out of there.

This chapter has also made me realize that I prefer single quotation marks to the more commonly accepted double quotation marks.

However, in homage to the octopus, I will be using eight quotation marks throughout the remainder of this chapter.

‘‘‘‘‘‘‘‘Octopi’’’’’’’’ may be incorrect, but its memory will live on. I also vow to print each one of these octo-quotation marks in octopus ink that I have milked myself.

I’m not sure if you can actually milk an octopus, but I plan on making it my life’s mission to find out.

Or, I could just Google it.

Which I did. Halfbakery.com raised similar questions, and also provided octopus ink-themed poetry and haiku, in case you were wondering.

A few other really bizarre links and videos come up when you Google ‘‘‘‘‘‘‘‘milking an octopus.’’’’’’’’

It does make me really sad, though, to find out that many cultures consider the incredibly intelligent octopus a delicacy. In Korea, you can order and eat a live octopus, cutting it up while it’s still alive and squirming. This, of course, is completely humane, much like our slaughterhouse methods here in the United States.

""""Don't Ask, Don't Tell"""" would be a good name for our attitudes toward cruelty to animals.

Octopuses (it still kills me to have to use this plural form) play games, use tools, practice observational learning, have been shown to possess both short-term and long-term memory, and have incredible maze and problem-solving skills. They can mimic other sea creatures. They are arguably the smartest invertebrate. Oh, and they taste delicious with teriyaki sauce.

Survival of the fittest, right? If I am able to kill it, I can, as long as I have a permit (sometimes). By this logic, I should be able to decide that Mr. Curtis, who lives on Stephens St., a block from my house, probably tastes delicious, and devour him.

Somehow, I always end up on these rants. This chapter began so innocuously. See what happens when the Greek language ruins all my fun? I get angry. Let that be a lesson to you.

Honestly, this is all Shaquille O'Neal's fault.

Upon returning from a visit to Greece, Shaq was asked if he had visited the Parthenon. He replied, "I don't know. I can't really remember the names of the clubs that we went to."

Greece was so incensed and offended at the disrespect shown it and its history by an international icon that it vowed revenge.

The country checked the history books and realized that trying to impose its will through the use of force doesn't work anymore (read up on the Roman and Ottoman Empires).

With its economy in shambles, Greece couldn't even buy any respect.

So, it was forced to turn to the only weapon it has: etymology.

Greece's sinister plan is to surreptitiously rescind the use of any non-Greek plurals in the English language, including 'octopi.' In doing so, it will cast a shadow of gloom over the lives of many Americans such as myself, whose only joy had been derived from the constant use of these fun words.

Within a few short years, we'll be begging at the sandaled feet of the Greeks for them to give us our linguistic sunshine back. We'll promise anything. We'll give them $11.1 billion in economic and security assistance. (Wait, we've already done that.) We'll go so far as to force Shaq and his declining skill set to finally retire and become a TV analyst. (Wait, I guess he already did.)

With nothing else to offer Greece, we as a nation will be forced even deeper into that inky Greek darkness.

I HAVE HAD A BABY WITH EVERY SINGLE DEFENDANT IN THE STATE OF OREGON.

Yesterday sucked.

Six words for you: Jury duty on absolutely no sleep.

I got home around eleven the night before last, and promptly took a sleeping pill and four melatonin pills. And then promptly lay awake in bed for the next seven and a half hours. Diphenhydramine didn't cut it. I should've tried some of diphenhydrayours.

That was a dumb joke.

There's a tight-knit community of insomniacs who post to Facebook in the middle of the night. It felt good to be a part of something bigger than myself.

I hate sunrises. Actually, there's nothing wrong with them per se, and I enjoy looking at sunrise pictures in coffee table books and the like just as much as the next guy. This morning's was actually particularly beautiful. But, it served as a visual aid to reinforce the point that my day was going to be a suckhole. Anytime I see a sunrise, I've either been up way too long or have had to get up way too early. In this morning's case, it was both.

I should be barred from recording songs that are named after natural phenomena that I have almost no firsthand experience with. "Sunrise" is obviously out, and I should probably also hold off on finishing my next hit single, "The Honduran Rain Of Fish."

I showed up to the jury room a fairly fashionable fifteen minutes late. Of course, I got the one remaining empty seat, next to the guy with whooping cough. Or consumption; I'm not sure. I don't have much firsthand experience with chronic wasting diseases, either.

There was a painting of a clown riding a carnival horse on the wall, and I wanted to rip it down and set it on fire, and then bawl my eyes out, just to make sure that everyone in the room knew how crappy I felt.

Leave No Childish Happiness Behind.

The State Of Oregon Judicial Department's introductory video, complete with poor acting and the requisite female African-American judge, was the first thing on the agenda. Actually, it was the only thing on the agenda. Then the waiting began.

We were informed that we should prepare to be there for the next nine to ten hours.

If picked for a trial, I would have literally gone to any length to make sure I didn't get selected for a jury.

"Yes, I'm wanted for six felonies in Mozambique. Yes, every single member of my family serves in law enforcement, even my cousin's unborn child. Yes, I have had a baby with every single defendant in the state of Oregon. Yes, I hate white people. Yes, I have IBS. Yes, I dine and dash, and then drink and drive."

If one of those six sentences didn't work, I contemplated faking a seizure. Or feigning Ebola. Or chanting "Start Tebow, Trade Sanchez" until they made me leave.

I pay taxes. I vote, even for county commissioners and pointless measures. I've never been on welfare. I even use the self-pay drop boxes when I visit state parks. Most of the time. What do you want from me, Oregon? (Cue annoyingly catchy Adam Lambert hit single here.)

Yes, I realize that without jurors the justice system wouldn't work fairly. But, there were at least 400 other able people in the waiting room, and it's safe to say that most, if not all, had gotten at least some sleep, and were therefore of more sound mind. Sounder mind? More soundlier mind?

My neighbor's whooping cough took a turn for the worse.

I've wished many times for a rewind button. Something I could press to give me a mulligan, to turn back time. But, a fast-forward button? For once, I would have been sorely tempted to use one.

I must be getting old. I used to pull all-nighters almost every week in college. Not to study, of course, but to have a ten-hour Lord Of The Rings marathon. Or a ten-hour Connect Four marathon (we actually did this). Or, to TP, egg, or otherwise 'beautify' various statues and security vehicles on campus (yup, we actually did this, too).

The aftermath of this all-nighter was different. I was a wreck, probably because I hadn't committed any misdemeanors or other mischievous acts during the night. My left eye was twitching. My head throbbed. My vision was blurred. Would I even have been able to tell if I were having a stroke?

I accidentally broke my juror badge. I came to the conclusion that this should be grounds for dismissal from duty. If I can't even be trusted with cheap plastic, how can I be trusted with a verdict?

I also attempted to slip a clerk $20 to let me go early. She wasn't impressed, and pointed out that she'd be happy to assign me to another room of the courthouse to stand trial for attempting to bribe a government employee.

Six hours passed.

My name was finally called, and I was released, my 'jury duty' complete. I, like hundreds of other people, had sat in a waiting room and done absolutely nothing, only to be sent home. Even if we only each get a check for $10 plus mileage, this scenario is played out daily in thousands of courtrooms across the nation. I think I'm beginning to see why our government has a budget deficit of $15 trillion.

What is the government doing to combat that deficit? Well, upon stumbling to my car, I found that, in addition to the $17 I'd already paid for parking, I had incurred a $40 parking ticket. My curbside receipt had fallen to the floor of my car.

Back to the courthouse tomorrow.

I love this country.

TOO MANY VOICES. NOT ENOUGH EARS.

I need to say something.

As I type, the profound words of a hit song are running through my head.

"Say what you need to say, say what you need to say."

Thanks for that, John Mayer. At least you probably never forget the words to that one when playing live.

According to my count, he utters the word 'say' exactly 75 times in this song. By all means, waste the next few minutes of your life figuring out if I'm right or wrong.

Unlike Mr. Mayer, what I need to say contains at least some subtle variance between clauses.

So what, you ask, do I really need to say?

No, I'm not a homosexual. Sorry, Andrew.

No, I don't have any STDs (yet), or a secret Angry Birds addiction.

No, I'm not a closet Republican, I'm not lactose intolerant, I don't know where Waldo is, and I haven't asked Jeeves.

Without further ado, here it is: I'm tired.

I'm not talking about the fact that I'm tired of John Mayer.

I'm not talking about sleep. I actually got a pretty restful six and a half hours of sleep last night, and faithfully imbibed my daily regimen of four cups of Colombian black coffee this morning.

No, it's something more than being physically exhausted.

Don't get me wrong: I've been busy. In the four days prior to the writing of this chapter, I played three shows, including one with Powerman 5000 (yes, they're still alive); played live on Portland's KGW Channel 8; made an in-store appearance at a record store; spent time tracking vocals at the studio; and made two live radio appearances. I also attempted to cram in some semblance of a social life. Oh, and I ate an almond.

So, needless to say, I haven't been sleeping enough. Mom, when you read this, save yourself the trouble of calling. I already know what you're going to say.

It's more than a need for REM, though. (I'm not talking about the music of REM. Nobody needs *that* anymore.) It's a need for peace. I feel like my soul is being worn thin.

When I first started playing music, it was something beautiful. Something meaningful, spiritual, cathartic.

While in college, I tried a little of everything (scholastically speaking), and I realized that music was the only thing that made me happy, that made me feel fulfilled.

Ever since then, I've been pursuing a dream of being a professional musician. My career started as a part-time drummer in a crappy garage band. I then sang and played guitar and bass for a couple of well-intentioned grunge bands before moving on to an acoustic pop band. I then became the singer and screamer in a hard rock/metal band. Next, I went solo, then joined an acoustic duo, then formed an alt/pop band.

I've been on twelve lengthy tours, had a tour van break down countless times, played in almost every US state and 5 countries, and had two songs on hundreds of FM stations. I've met some amazing people, fans and musicians alike, played with some pretty big names, and sold more records than I ever thought I would. And I don't regret any of it so far.

Somewhere, though, in all of this, the simple joy of playing music has all but disappeared. Gone the way of LeBron James' shot in 4th quarters of NBA Finals games.

It's a business, folks. I am an entrepreneur in one of the world's most cutthroat industries. To ignore the business aspect of a music career is to kiss your aspirations goodbye. No tongue, please.

Life, in fact, is a business, and everyone is selling something.

Usually, it's oneself. It happens on an interpersonal level, day in and day out. We all want to be noticed, valued, loved. And so we sell ourselves.

I'm not talking about selling oneself for money, although you hookers and indentured servants out there will identify with that. I'm talking about proving ourselves, getting people to notice, getting people to buy into what we're trying to be. It happens in the workplace. We sell ourselves, pushing our own agendas to get a raise, a promotion. More important letters after our names. A lunch break, even.

I do it too. In this crazy music business, it seems impossible to get ahead without selling yourself, unless you can pay the right people to sell you. All I really want to do is to write and play music, to travel, to meet people. It never turns out to be that simple. In the ever-burgeoning music scene, every artist, every band, is striving to sell themselves on what they have that's different. That's new. That will change your life. A chord, a rhyme, a tattoo, a haircut, a hook, a look, a downloadable album that you can pick your price for.

There are too many voices, and not enough ears.

But the voices rarely take this into consideration. Instead, they babble on.

Of course, I wouldn't mind having millions of fans, multiple platinum albums, and the last name Mars. I'd even take two out of those three. It's so easy to fall into the trap of wanting more, and to forget to be grateful for the people I know, the shows I've played, the fans who have connected with a lyric I've written. To be grateful for a show in Cave Junction, OR, in the middle of nowhere, in a dive bar, that by all of the standards of the industry was a worthless show, but where I met some amazing, giving, hilarious people with stories to tell.

Who am I? I'm a guy with a voice, a guitar, and a band. One of tens of thousands of such guys. Millions, maybe. How should I sell myself and my band to separate my voice from the rest? I don't know. I wish I didn't have to figure it out.

I haven't written any songs lately. I feel like my proverbial well has run dry. Worse, I'm in an industry where wells are frowned upon, shunned; where everyone is forced to hook up to city water to survive. The same blandly reliable city water that everyone else on your street is drinking. No wells. No waterfalls. No flash floods. Just a faucet and a knob.

I can't remember the last time that I actually had the chance to sit down somewhere beautiful and play my guitar. And sing. To myself, to God, to whatever varmints might be listening.

I want to rediscover the spark, the passion, the purpose of playing music. Why am I doing it? Why do I spend seventy hours a week on something that doesn't satisfy? Should I be pouring my energies into something else? Or taking a different approach to the music business? Or take some time off? Or keep my schedule jam-packed in the hopes that things will work themselves out? Time and life are not renewable resources.

I love my band. I love my fans and friends. I love my manager, my attorney, and especially my PR coordinator. I love being on stage. I love traveling. I love meeting new people every day. I love Russell Stafford. (There, I said it.) Don't get me wrong: there's still plenty that I love about what I do. I simply never wanted it to turn into just another job, albeit one with killer benefits.

What's it all for, anyway?

You would think that winning three Super Bowls would be enough to provide meaning and fulfillment. In an insightful interview with

60 Minutes, Tom Brady acknowledged that he was still searching for something more meaningful than all his accomplishments.

Somehow I suspect that even if Wes Welker would have caught that pass and the Patriots would have pulled out a win in Super Bowl XLVI, Brady still wouldn't have found what he was looking for in his fourth ring.

I sometimes wish that happiness and fulfillment were more cut-and-dry. I sometimes wish that success would do a better job of providing them. Even though I haven't reached the level of success that I'm striving for, I'd at least know that amaranthine happiness was waiting for me when I got there.

I'm starting to realize, though, that the things in life that *do* satisfy are things that don't show up at the finish line. Or in a paycheck, a resumé, even an obituary.

They show up in a friendship. A song. A sunset. A promise that one day every tear of emptiness and nonfulfillment will be wiped from our eyes.

Ambition, in and of itself, isn't wrong. However, so often weeds of aspiration choke out the roses that we never stopped to smell.

The famed British poet Walter Savage Landor put it like this: "Ambition has but one reward for all: A little power, a little transient fame; a grave to rest in, and a fading name."

I'm going to go for a walk tomorrow. Alone. With my guitar.

One mortal voice and two immortal ears will be more than enough.

IT'S A PERRY THING.

I swore I would avoid writing about politics.

However, I've already expressed my controversial views on cauliflower and on octopus rights, so why not piss a few more people off?

While I'm in the process of making people angry, this would also be a good time to admit that I absolutely despise Journey. "Don't Stop Believin'" is one of the worst songs ever written, and absolutely the worst possible karaoke selection. At least Steve Perry could hit the notes. You, Mr. Drunken Karaoke Rock Star, cannot.

Now that I've alienated 75 percent of America, I'll turn my focus to the Tea Party.

I could write an entire book on why I ridicule you and all the inconsistencies that make up your ideology, Tea Partiers. But, mercifully, I'll limit my scope to a single point.

At a Republican presidential debate in September 2011, Texas' execution of 234 inmates during Rick Perry's time as governor drew some of the loudest applause of the night.

The crowd also applauded when Ron Paul was asked if he would let an uninsured person die on the hospital floor. Even most *Republicans* in America cringed.

Ah, you silly Tea Partiers. Don't you want less government? Smaller government? Yet you want to give your government the right to take life, to execute, and to do it frequently, even capriciously. Is there any right or power we can provide our government that is bigger than this?

Good thing Rick Perry isn't asked to remember and list the inmates on death row before they are executed. "What's the third one, there? Let's see…"

It seems to me that the only common denominator here, Tea Party, is that you are pro-death. Do the math: you're pro-capital punishment, pro-war, pro-gun rights, pro-abandonment of the uninsured. But God forbid that you kill an unborn child. They could grow up to be a Republican, and you need their vote.

If your beliefs fit neatly on a bumper sticker, you need to think harder.

It must be a Perry thing. Coincidentally, I also hate Tyler Perry. Oh, Lawd. And don't even get me started on Katy.

Stephen Perry's alright in my book, though. In case you don't know, he's the British inventor of the rubber band. Arguably the greatest thing a Perry has ever done. Prove me wrong, and I'll buy you a Perrier.

FROM ACCORDION TO ZITHER.

It's true.

The only things that an indie band needs to succeed these days are a couple of cardigans and a really weird instrument. Something that doesn't even qualify as an instrument on most people's lists. A trash can lid, a fork, or an orphan. Something that fell out of the engine of their minivan or the drivetrain of their bike on the way to the show.

I am intrigued by recent musical instrumentation trends. Not only are household objects being converted to instruments, but a whole slew of ancient and/or obscure instruments are being resuscitated.

Everything from accordion to zither.

I love weird instruments. I own a mandolin, which, based on its first syllable, is arguably the most masculine instrument. I've screwed around on hammer dulcimers, glockenspiels, sackbuts, and lap steels, and am known to just crush it on kazoo.

I have always wanted a flügelhorn. Mainly just for the name. Hope you're reading this, Santa. I've been really good.

However, there are certain instruments that should be shot on sight.

The definition of a gentleman? Someone who can play the bagpipes, but chooses not to.

And, didgeridoos? Really, Australia? All that blowing for just one crappy note? How about you didgeri*don't*.

These bamboo trunks masquerading as instruments were frequently used by Occupy protesters in cities across the US. This pretty much says it all.

For my next solo album, I'm going to mic my stomach and capture the gurgling. This sound is properly termed *borborygmus*. Don't ask me why I know this.

Then, I'm going to add some tribal drums and market it as a didgeridoo instrumental concept piece. It will undoubtedly go platinum Down Under.

I will celebrate my accomplishments by drinking a Foster's, putting some shrimp on the barbie with a three-foot hunting knife, and starring in my own outdoor adventure show.

Crikey!

Of course, to have a platinum album in Australia, you only need to sell 70,000 copies. I can piss 70,000 copies. True story.

So, here's my advice to you, Mr. Indie Musician: Choose a weird instrument. By all means. But, choose wisely, or I will punch you right in the mustache.

MILLIONS OF MISERLY LIVERS.

There are three types of people.

Don't believe anything you've read before. Ever. This is how it breaks down.

First, there are people who don't give a rat's ass. Or any other part of the rat, for that matter. They're especially selfish with rat spleens, which, to be fair, are delicious with a little barbecue sauce.

Self-absorbed, self-sufficient: this group tells Haiti that building their capital city on a fault line was arguably the dumbest decision in history (with the possible exception of giving Flavor Flav his own reality show). They also say things like "God hates French" and have bumper stickers that read "Obama: Not MY president." Reality check: if you live in America, America's president is *your* president. Whether you're a Republican or a Democrat, whether you think he's a god or the Antichrist, whether you think beef stroganoff is a food or a herd of masturbating cattle, we don't get to pick who our president is *after* they've been elected.

Your only options are to deal with it or to pull a Peter Griffin and secede. Or go hunting with Dick Cheney and hope for the worst.

Second, there's a large group of people that sends a check to the Red

Cross. Members of this group have three books of "First Class Forever" stamps in their glove boxes. Their hearts are bigger than their work boots. Actually, they probably don't own a pair. Sorry, ladies, but Gucci Pratos don't count. This group might look for the easiest way to help, but who says easy can't be effective? (Just ask a hooker.) Case in point: U.S. cellphone users donated almost $32 million to the American Red Cross via text message in the Haiti earthquake aftermath.

Kids, if you're ever caught texting in class, you now have a killer excuse.

Third, there is a small group of people who are the hands and feet of relief efforts. Well over two years after the Haiti earthquake, they're still there. It's crazy to me to think of being 'on call' for the Red Cross or a similar organization, ready to drop everything at a moment's notice to place oneself in harm's way. Why? Because somebody, somewhere, is suffering.

In case you're wondering, I belong to Grupo Numero Dos.

Yes, I studied Spanish in college. Want to learn a cool phrase? Try this: "Jon Davidson es asombroso. Compre su nuevo álbum." Teach it to all your friends!

Growing up, I thought 'manual labor' was the work involved in changing gears in a stick shift car. For two months following the Haiti earthquake, we of Crown Point donated all the proceeds from ticket, album, and merch sales at our shows to the American Red Cross. I'm happy to say we raised several thousand dollars, but that's just a drop in a Carnie Wilson-sized bucket.

What is an injured, starving Haitian going to do with a dollar bill? Stores are closed, damaged, looted. Dollar bills are low in nutrients, and you can't live off of the blow they invariably contain for all that long.

I would love to be in group 3.

Maybe someday, I keep telling myself. Maybe when the next über-disaster rolls around. Right now, I have too much on my plate, and bigger, more accommodating plates are costly and hard to come by.

I think of the fact that I don't have any formal training in medicine or disaster response, and that my tetanus shot is as out of date as everything Hinder has ever done. I tell myself that I would just be 'in the way'.

I weigh 165 pounds. Who or what, exactly, would I be getting in the way of?

In the case of Haiti, all the money in Halliburton's Cayman Islands account wouldn't make a difference if there was nobody available to administer supplies, to pass out food, to keep order, to give medical care.

Membership in group 3 is coveted, revered. It's more MLB All-Star, less Pro Bowl. It seems to be the most tangible, hands-on way to bring help to the helpless. However, just as there can be no group 2 without a group 3, there can be no group 3 without a group 2. You group 2-timers know who you are. Have you texted "HAITI" and "JAPAN" and "REDCROSS" to your cellphone provider? Have you rounded off to the nearest dollar at the supermarket? If so, I commend you. If I were wearing a hat, I would tip it. If I were wearing a dress, there's a small chance I'd even curtsey if you asked nicely.

When you're giving, the way that you give becomes almost irrelevant. Don't feel like you're doing less with a cellphone than someone else is doing with a stethoscope and a bag of blood. We may have taken the easy road, but our job is important, too.

According to the Haitian government, the 2010 earthquake caused an estimated 316,000 fatalities, and disease, starvation and a lack of medical care pushed the death toll even higher.

This means that over 105 times as many people died in Haiti than did in 9/11. Imagine 105 9/11 attacks merged into one cataclysm and you'll get a picture of the suffering and loss that has taken place.

105.

316,000. Most in mass graves.

9/11 was a terrible tragedy, to be sure, and I don't make this comparison to turn it into some inopportune yet minor contretemps. Obviously it wasn't a natural disaster but rather an event caused by humanity, which places it in a different category altogether. However, I'm just trying to enumerate what took place in Haiti in a tangible way.

I also am not focusing on Haiti to somehow diminish the tragedies that have taken place since, in disparate places like Japan and Joplin. However, Haiti's death toll was so staggeringly high, and the country's access to resources so limited, that I feel that Haiti's earthquake is appropriately indicative of the untold suffering that both natural and manmade disasters can cause.

Just because this tragedy has already faded from our collective consciousness and been replaced by new headlines and new disasters doesn't mean that all the problems have been solved, needs have been met, or even that all the bodies have been found.

The people of New Orleans know that even seven years after Katrina, there is still work to be done. We spent a night there on tour a year and a half ago, and we were shocked to find that whole neighborhoods are still in shambles, while Bourbon Street parties on night after night in drunken revelry. Millions of dollars of potential aid are drunk and filtered out by millions of miserly livers.

The $32 million Americans donated to Haiti relief looks pretty puny next to the $90 *billion* Americans spend on alcohol consumption alone. Annually.

However, it's been heartwarming to hear about countless individuals who have given and given to help people they've never met. America as a nation has definitely made a myriad of mistakes, from foreign policy to internal affairs. But let's not overlook the incredible magnanimity of its citizens.

Charity is synonymous with humanity. We can't wait around for the right time to join group 3. Sure, it would be ideal if we all could immediately catch a flight to Haiti, Japan, or Joplin. Eritrea, Tuscaloosa, or the Philippines.

But, just because dropping everything isn't an option right now doesn't mean that we of group 2 don't have work to do. We can pick up a pen and write a check. Pick up our phones and text. Donate blood. Clothes. Goods. Organs.

To avoid potential lawsuits, my lawyer has advised me to include the caveat that you should probably wait to donate organs until you've died.

What's important is that we do *something*. People are still counting on us.

LIVE LIKE WE'RE MAYAN.

The Doomsday Clock is ticking.

It's 2012. This year, according to interpretations of an ancient Mayan tablet, the world will end.

It will end in very similar fashion to when it also ended at Y2K and twice in 2011, according to Harold Camping.

You'd think that the Mayans, with all their alleged prophetic knowledge, would have been able to accurately foretell the catastrophic, mysterious downfall of their own civilization.

Funny thing is, the Mayans aren't the stupid ones. We are.

The Mayan 'long-count' calendar (actually, there are several) doesn't predict the end of the world. Yes, the 13th Baktun ends on 12/21/12. However, a time of great celebration is supposed to ensue, not Armageddon. (Armayageddon?) Does your world end every time you celebrate a birthday? It may feel like it has when you wake up the next morning, but in most cases you're still very much alive.

Furthermore, the Mayans make many references to dates that occur past 2012. Many Mayans are still alive today, and they're not freaking out about this year. The whole idea was coined by New Age author José Argüelles in 1987. Yup, I've been alive longer than this whole 2012 Doomsday thing. Yup, Snoop Dogg has been high nonstop for longer than this whole 2012 Doomsday thing.

Once upon a time, I had a good-natured friend named Greta. She bought a tome about the Zodiac, and asked me what my sign was. "Sagittarius," I said. She proceeded to read me two pages about myself and how my sign interacted with hers, about how I was a natural-born leader, about how I had some inner pain that hadn't yet been dealt with. She punctuated many a sentence with exclamations of how spot-on the book's interpretation was.

I let her finish before I casually informed her that I'm actually a Libra.

"Oh," she muttered, crestfallen, and left the room.

Reminds me of an episode of *Criss Angel Mindfreak* in which Criss poses as a tarot card reader in Vegas. Once his subjects have been blindfolded, he swaps out the tarot card and instead reads the same paragraph from the cheesiest small-town newspaper horoscope to each person, telling them how they are strong yet have a need to be loved, among other generic, widely applicable truisms. Many of his subjects start crying and tell him that he's able to see into their souls more than even their loved ones can.

At the end of the episode, he lets people in on his little secret: they've been duped.

We all share in this human experience. We all need love; we all have love to give. We all want attention. We all take dumps which often stink.

Mine stink less than yours. Being a vegetarian, I don't have ten pounds of rotting carcass in my colon.

No Chichen Itza for this guy. Although a Mayan city, it sounds quite edible.

Everybody merely wants someone to reinforce what they already believe to be true. Why do the best psychiatrists merely listen? Why do people pay thousands to talk to them? It's crazy: psychiatrists make more than Bernie Madoff. Well, more than he makes *now,* anyways.

Everybody wants to be heard. I once read about a guy who made a comfortable living on the streets of Tokyo by charging people money in exchange for letting them yell at him.

Everybody wants a framework to explain why life is the way it is, and someone to blame when things go wrong.

Americans spend $200 million a year on astrology. I am clearly in the wrong profession.

"Pluto is no longer a planet! How else am I supposed to explain the powerful pull on my psyche?"

I cannot tell you how ridiculously inane it is to me when people try and quantify human interaction through the use of Zodiac signs. "Ah, he dumped me because I'm a Taurus and he's a Cancer. It had to be because the Sun was in transit to my natal Saturn, and..." Really? You sure? None of this happened because you are a crazy biznatch? Of course not; let's blame some stars.

I am going to become an astrologer. That way, nothing is ever my fault.

The reason this book sucks so hard is because I wrote it while there was a stellium, or buildup of planets in Libra.

It has nothing to do with the fact that I'm a mediocre writer with a penchant for tangents, sesquipedalianisms and run-on sentences.

Screw it; maybe I'll look into gender-specific psychiatry. Men don't talk, as a general rule, unless it's about sports. Or women. But, of course, never women's sports. Über-lame.

I'll just charge women $200 an hour to complain about their problems. The best part about listening to women is that they don't even *want* you to find a solution! Solve their issues, and they have to go to all the trouble of finding new things to complain about.

Or, maybe I'll just become a doomsday prophet. Mr. Camping may look like a fool now, but at least he looks like a very wealthy fool. Everyone in the Bible Belt will be getting thank-you cards this Christmas.

The best part about Camping's prediction, and other Christian doomsday predictions, is this: Matthew 24:36 states that no one knows the day or the hour when the world will end. No one except God. Well, God and Harold Camping, that is.

The truth is that the end will come for all of us someday. It won't come this year for most of us, but it may come sooner than that for you. For me. For someone we care about.

As much as I hate to quote yet another American Idol star, there's truth in Kris Allen's one and only hit single. "We only got 86,400 seconds in a day to turn it all around or throw it all away....gotta live like we're dying."

Let's also not forget to live like we're Mayan. In other words, relax. The world is not ending this year.

MOUNTAIN BIKING THE AMISH WAY.

I just finished an epic mountain bike ride.

Yes, the word 'epic' is so 2010. But, I'm the one writing this book, not you. Shut up.

Anyway, five clear Portland December days in a row are about as rare as an old British guy with all his teeth. Like, actually still in his mouth. I knew I had to take advantage of this ephemeral dry singletrack.

As a result of the clear skies, though, it's been ridiculously cold the last week or so. It's currently an intolerable 42° Fahrenheit outside. All of our friends and fans in North Dakota and Saskatchewan are scoffing as they read this.

However, once you factor in the wind chill from the east wind blowing in from the Columbia Gorge, and Oregon's extremely high barometric Berscheid factor...

OK, I'm just a sissy. There's no such thing as the Berscheid factor. Yet.

In any case, I knew it was best to bundle up before heading out to face such bleak conditions. I glanced at myself in the mirror before walking out the door.

Brown North Face fleece. Black snowboarding gloves. The svelte fuzzy grey beanie-under-red-bike-helmet combo.

Khaki shorts. White tube socks. Blue thermal underwear. Long jons, if you please.

Anytime I can write 'long' and 'jon' in the same phrase, I will.

I was a walking (well, riding) fashion faux pas. For a guy who refuses to brush his teeth with a toothbrush that doesn't match his shirt, this outfit was the Titanic on a collision course with the iceberg of Goodwill. I was tempted to ride there and literally donate everything I was wearing. However, naked bike rides aren't even that much fun during the summer, and we all know what cold weather does to the male anatomy. No more long jon.

However, as pneumonia also isn't on my bucket list, I wasn't too concerned with my appearance as I rode the trails of Powell Butte. It was a great ride, by the way. I only saw one other foolhardy biker on the trail, and he looked even more ridiculous than I did. So, of course, I laughed at him.

I will gladly sacrifice style any day for the sake of something I love. So will most people, I think. Did those businessmen I was watching the Oregon-Oregon State game with last night really, firmly believe that those Beavers neckties were the perfect match for their light blue Oxford shirts?

Actually, sadly, they probably did.

As I was pedaling down 174th St. to get to the trailhead, I passed an Amish man in a horse and buggy. This would've been a commonplace sight in the Midwest where I grew up, but I'm pretty sure this guy was a long way from home. Still, he waved and smiled as I blew past him on my Trek 8700 carbon-fiber 27-speed mountain bike.

I could take him head-to-head in a gentlemanly race any day. All you strapping young Amish lads can take that as a direct challenge. Ponies only, though, please.

Do you know the reason why Amish men shave their mustaches? Contrary to popular belief, it's not because they are enamored with Abraham Lincoln. On the contrary, it's because the mustache is, in their minds, an emblem of war and the military, involvement in which they are morally opposed to. Personally, I think that beards without mustaches look pretty weird. They look even weirder if the wearer also has a unibrow, but that's a whole different story.

At least the Amish can compensate for their emasculating lack of a flavor saver with those über-pimp top hats, and by knowing that tourism brings in a cool $30,000 annually, per capita, to many Amish towns.

The Amish have actually had a long history of sacrifice for the sake of what they love and believe. The Amish people originated in 16th century Switzerland out of the Anabaptist movement. Anabaptists believed that everyone named Ana should be able to choose what they believed for themselves. Although all the Anas had been baptized as infants, they were re-baptized as adults, once they were old enough to make their own decisions. For this, they were oppressed and sometimes killed, yet they clung to their beliefs.

While I certainly don't champion all of Amish ideology, they must be doing something right. Their simple, hardworking lifestyle, free from most of the pressures and strictures of modern American society, attracts many new converts every year, and their numbers continue to grow across North America.

Due in large part, I trust, to those über-pimp top hats.

This really could be the first piece of literature ever written that encompasses both mountain biking and the Amish. In one chapter, nonetheless. I'm not sure how I got here. I guess, though, that it all comes full circle: the Amish can and do indeed ride bikes. They've even developed a line of über-pimp top hat bike helmets.

I have no idea if this is true, but I desperately want it to be.

I think it would be fun to be Amish for a day. Hopefully not on a day where a whole lot of manual labor was getting done. My management's contract contains a strict anti-barn-building clause.

It's crazy to me how much of society views the Amish culture in a negative light. People have taken to pelting Amish carriages with rocks. This ended tragically in the case of one six-month-old North Carolina Amish girl who was struck in the head by a rock and died from her injuries. Another Canadian Amish woman also required thousands of dollars of reconstructive surgery after being hit in the face by a beer bottle from a passing car.

Just because we as a society view another culture or group as weird doesn't give us the right to trample on their rights. Amish people are among the most peaceful, most family-oriented, most hardworking people in existence. And they certainly aren't the backwards, ignorant individuals that Hollywood and TV often portray them as. They don't view all technology as evil, but simply look at each new technological advance in an objective light to see if it will bring their families and community together, or drag them further apart.

Plus, arguably their most famous and dreaded criminal's most heinous crime was that of forcefully shaving off the beards of his Amish compatriots.

I'm not sure how I ended up on this pro-Amish soapbox. (Can the Amish even *use* soap?) I honestly can't say that I even know any Amish people. However, I admire their commitment to what they believe, and admire their sense of community and harmony. I admire the fact that they've willingly sacrificed many of the so-called 'comforts' that we enjoy in order to preserve the things that are most important to them.

Would I want to be Amish? No way. Is there something to be learned from their way of life? Most definitely.

Would even a polite young Amish girl laugh at what I'm still wearing as I write this? By all means.

LOSS.

I lost my microphone.

It's an Audix OM7. Nothing special, but it's a pretty good mic. It's Absolut, but not quite Belvedere. Pippen, but not quite Jordan. Dog, but not quite cat. Nonetheless, it's my mic, and I love the way it sounds.

I lost it at a festival in Portland ten days ago. Taken by another band? Perhaps. Why a singer would want to make out with a black piece of man-plastic that has been all up on another dude's lips is beyond me. To me, my microphone is like my earwax: meant for my mouth, and my mouth only.

Just for the record, I don't actually eat my earwax. I broke that habit six weeks ago. I've been faithfully attending EA meetings ever since.

In any case, I've been forced to use my backup microphone at my last three shows. Making the switch has been like switching from wearing underwear to wearing bubble wrap in its stead: it still works, but it's kind of noisy at inopportune times.

I've sent out emails to every staff member at the festival, every sound person, every other band. I've even put up "Missing" signs on telephone poles, and I roam the streets at night calling its name.

I have a sinking feeling it's not coming home.

My devastating loss, coupled with some other pressing matters involving aspects of my career that are beyond my control, was weighing on my mind as I checked my email yesterday afternoon. I was bombarded with the news of the devastation caused by Tropical Storm Washi, and the 1,257 lives it claimed. Come on, world, I'm trying to have a pity party here. Who invited the Philippines?

I have to be honest: nothing puts a missing microphone on the back burner like the tale of a mother desperately searching for her missing 12-year-old daughter, using her bare hands to pull apart the wreckage. The woman told reporters that her daughter's face and voice kept appearing in her mind constantly throughout the night.

A couple years ago, I wrote a song called "Sound Of Your Voice" that ended up on Crown Point's first album. I've lost way too many people that I love, including an uncle to cancer a couple years ago and a college friend to suicide last year. My fondest memories of the loved ones I've lost often involve the sound of their voices: the way they laughed, the way they said their trademark jokes and phrases.

A line from the song's first verse: "Silence is waiting, reiterating that life and loss are one."

Somewhere in between the story of the earthquakes and that of Tuesday's killer tsunami, I stopped thinking about my microphone. Sure, I'm bummed about it. But in the grand scheme, it's a pretty nominal thing to lose.

It's as if the server forgot the artichokes on my pizza. Do I love artichokes? You bet. Will I stand up on a table in the middle of the restaurant, rip my shirt, and fling soup spoons at the server? Definitely. Will I drench a hapless onlooker at a nearby table with Grenache because *they* got artichokes? Of course!

Did that really happen? I plead the fifth.

But in the end, artichokes or no artichokes, I can still sleep at night. Even if it's in jail.

Everyone I know has misplaced something at least once. I have a friend who lost a rental car in Vegas somehow, and another who to this day doesn't know where one of her teeth is. I realized recently that I've been keeping the spare set of keys for my car in my car. Not my best work.

I also lost a good portion of the manuscript of this book due to a corrupt drive and the fact that I failed to back the file up in an alternate location. All of the hilarious and poignant words I'd written? Gone forever. I had to scramble to replace them with all these crappy chapters (crapters?) that you're now being forced to endure.

All things considered, though, it's tempting to regard trivial loss as more than it is. Microphones can be replaced. People cannot.

Why must loss and tragedy be so intrinsic to our existence?

Some questions don't have easy answers. At least not yet.

I want to be available; I want to be able to interrupt my own agenda to reach out to someone who has lost someone or something important. I want to spend some time with them, and admit that I don't know what to say. I want to be there to offer a prayer, give a hug, and ask them what I can do to help them make it through.

Sometimes, I succeed at fulfilling these ideals. Sometimes, I fail.

Loss can be devastating. It can also be an opportunity for healing to take place. In the midst of loss, I hope that I can help those in my life who are suffering gain peace and a little hope.

WARNING: YOU ARE STUPID.

Breakfast.

As I finished my bowl of Wheat Chex this morning, Minisaurus hopped up on my lap, curled up, and immediately fell asleep. I had things to do. I tried moving her a couple times, and she responded by glaring at me and attempting to bite off my fingers. She then re-curled up and promptly resumed snoring.

So, trapped at the kitchen table with no electronic devices to entertain me, I was forced to resort to an antiquated pastime: reading.

All that I had at my disposal was the Wheat Chex box.

After perusing the back panel, which of course was laden with the usual information about how great whole grains are for me and how they reduce my risk of heart disease, baldness, leprosy, and just generally being uncool, I turned to the Nutrition Facts and ingredients panel. There, in bold and capital letters, I saw the following statement:

ALLERGY WARNING: CONTAINS WHEAT.

Yes, I know we've all heard the stories of the woman who sued McDonald's because her coffee cup didn't inform her that her coffee would be hot. But really? There's wheat in Wheat Chex? Now you tell me, General Mills, as I rapidly slip into anaphylactic shock. Why didn't you just simply put the word wheat in the name of the cereal or something?

Sometimes, America, I just have to shake my head, smile, and move on.

As long as I don't move on to make a PB&J. Turns out, according to its label's own allergy warning, that the peanut butter I was about to spread contains peanuts. Who knew?

DEAR DAD.

I can't actually address this chapter to my dad.

I doubt he'll read this book anytime soon. It's not available in hardcover, and is about as far from a scholarly work as you can get. I don't even provide footnotes for the 'facts' that I mainly Googled.

I guess we're even. I've only read two of the eleventeen books he's written. I'm waiting for the movies to come out.

Also, he's in Romania for a month. This is good and bad news: Bad because I don't actually get to talk to him on Father's Day, but good because I have a little extra time to send something to his home in Michigan and still have him think the gift was on time. I think he's still waiting for last year's Father's Day gift too, but I'm not sure.

I refuse to buy ties for Father's Day. I think the tie industry is being kept afloat year after year by countless thousands of unimaginative American drones who are convinced that their dad wants, even needs, yet another garish American flag tie. You know you're guilty. (It's also kept afloat by cheap slave labor overseas, but I'll save that rant for another day.)

Now, Father's Day ties come with a personal touch. Several online retailers are offering ties with the photo of your choice printed on them. Your picture, his picture, a picture of Ron Jeremy...the choice is yours. Whatever you do, don't send him a tie with a cartoon of the prophet Muhammad on it.

I've been blessed with a world-class dad. He's one of the most patient, intelligent, funny, wise, faith-filled, well-balanced people I've ever met. We've climbed at least one mountain together every year since I was old enough to carry a backpack (which, in my family, was around the age of four months).

The best thing about my dad is that he never tried to make my decisions for me. He taught me right and wrong through the way he lived.

I admire the way he's always been so real, so transparent.

I've seen him cry when one of our pets died.

I've seen him scream and curse when our brand-new Ping-Pong table flew off the top of our van and smashed onto the pavement of I-80.

I've been demolished by his scathing backhand on the tennis court. He'll still be kicking my butt from a wheelchair in 30 years.

I've seen him, year after year, simply love God, my mom, my sister, and me in a remarkable way.

Good dads are hard to come by. Trust me, I've checked craigslist.

In the words of that timeless commercial: Dad, you're my dad, and I love you man! This book's for you.

IGNORANCE: NOT ALWAYS BLISS.

Swine flu.

It's still out there. In August 2010, the World Health Organization declared the pandemic officially over. And, right on cue, another outbreak took place in Venezuela in April 2011, and a new strain of H1N1 cropped up in Iowa in January 2012.

At least it won't be in Egypt anytime soon. As you've probably heard, the mercurial Egyptian government ordered the slaughter of all 300,000 pigs in the country in 2009.

Unfortunately, they failed to simply Google 'swine flu.' Had they, they would've realized that swine flu is currently being transmitted from human to human. You're not going to get it from swine at this point. Not by eating a pig, dancing with a pig, or even cuddling with a pig a little bit, provided you take them out for dinner first.

Ignorance, it seems, is not always bliss, especially for these 300,000 swine, and for the farmers whose livelihood depended on them.

The World Organization for Animal Health says that "there is no evidence of infection in pigs, nor of humans acquiring infection directly from pigs." This hasn't stopped China, Russia, Ukraine, and other nations from banning pork exports from Mexico. Why would you import pork (impork?) from Mexico, anyway? Unless, of course, there are illicit drugs hidden somewhere inside.

There's also the case of the mistaken mushrooms. Several years ago, a Colorado newspaper published photos of Paddy-Straw mushrooms in their Food section, encouraging people to use them in certain recipes. Several of their readers went out and found some Paddy-Straws, ate them, and promptly died. Apparently, the newspaper had mistakenly published photos of the similar-looking, yet highly toxic, Death Cap mushroom. I'm sure the newspaper staff was encouraged, at least, to know that people still read the paper.

I thought about this as I was eating a mushroom rice bowl at Portland's newest high-rise dining establishment, Departure, the other day. These mushrooms were delicious, but the Death Caps probably were, too. At least I hope so: it would suck to have a crappy last meal right before the nausea, vomiting, abdominal pain, diarrhea, and death set in.

Ever think about the etymology of certain words? Take 'mushroom,' for example. What does it mean? That there's room for mush inside of them? Or is it named after a mythical room to which mothers send their boisterous children to eat their mush when they've misbehaved? Then there's the word 'cockpit.' I don't think I even want to know.

I digress.

The moral of all this is simple: ignorance is not always bliss. Our global society is so quick to take action that we often fail to fully comprehend what's going on. The invasion of Iraq would be a prime example of this, as would the deadly yet FDA-approved drug Ketek from 2005. Sometimes, in a rush to make things right, we end up doing the wrong things.

Let's hope the next deadly influenza strain isn't dubbed 'baby flu.'

WATER BALLOONS OVER AFGHANISTAN.

Chocolate can make people do some crazy things.

Yesterday, as I watched some kids run roughshod through their lawn, ruthlessly trampling the slow and the weak among them in search of those ubiquitous pastel candy-filled Easter eggs, I calmly reached for a bag of Hershey's Kisses. Dark chocolate. I am a grown-up, and therefore I got to eat as much candy as I wanted without even having to look for it.

I got to thinking: when was the last time I hunted for Easter eggs? Was I eight? Nine?

Granted, I've had some success hiding eggs for various kids over the years. What kid would ever think to look in the toilet? In the litter box? I was just trying to help these kids curtail their sugar intake, after all.

So why don't we adults hunt for Easter eggs anymore? Perhaps it's because the experience doesn't more closely resemble big game hunting. "If I don't get to drink Hamm's with the guys and kill things while I'm hunting these Easter eggs, you can count me out."

Or, perhaps the eggs wouldn't meet any need in our life, and the hunt wouldn't fit into our schedule. "If these Easter eggs don't come with 370 HD channels, a lottery ticket, and a weight-loss pill, then I'm not gonna waste my time looking."

What is it about growing older that makes us unable to experience the joy we once found in simple things? Why does everything have to have a reason? When did childish fun lose its appeal? Why don't we adults have pillow fights? Or play freeze tag? Or 'doctor?' Okay, perhaps we still play doctor, but simply call it something else.

Instead, we adults spend our time slaving away at jobs we never wanted, saving up for the vacation that never turns out the way we hoped it would. We fight wars, we fight at home, we fight at work. What if every disagreement was settled with water guns? What if every war was waged with Super Soakers? What if these deranged individuals I can't stop hearing about on the news stormed into churches and retirement homes and schools and office buildings, twin CPS 4100s in hand, and opened fire, simply drenching hordes of innocent people? What if CNN News was full of reports of American fighter jets dropping thousands of water balloons upon unsuspecting Afghanistan?

"Unless you change and become like little children, you will not enter Heaven…"

I'm not trying to trivialize the world's problems. I'm just saying that maybe if we learned to stop once in a while, put away our investment portfolios and our iPhones, and enjoy an Easter egg hunt, the world would be a better place.

SIMPLY OFFAL.

Please pass the tripe.

It makes sense to me that if you're going to needlessly kill an animal to begin with, you might as well use as much of it as you can.

However, the Indians did this, and look where it got them.

When I say 'Indians', of course, I mean the politically-incorrect, yet still prevalent, term for Native Americans. A term that white people gave them *after* realizing that they weren't Indian. This makes perfect sense, considering actual Indians and Native Americans look absolutely nothing alike. But, the victor writes the history books. The name has stuck.

I think we're afraid that if we use the term Native Americans, our kids might figure out that we weren't actually here first, and that we did some pretty despicable things to get our grubby white hands on this once-beautiful land.

Plus, Cleveland Native Americans is a pretty cumbersome name for a baseball team.

Am I the only one who thinks that the Cleveland Indians' logo is unbelievably racist? Not to mention the fact that we still have an NFL team called the Redskins. I think that the AAI would have some unsportsmanlike things to say if a professional franchise's name still contained the word 'yellow' in reference to skin color.

What does this have to do with tripe? Not much. How did my brain arrive at this point? Not sure.

In case tripe has never been all up in your mouth, or in case it has, you should know that it's derived from the stomachs of various animals.

Not gross enough for you? Try green tripe. No, it's not the new eco-friendly tripe, but rather the unwashed variety, so it contains some of whatever an animal ate last before it was slaughtered.

Apparently, dogs love it, so it's used in many pet foods.

Wikipedia lists 62 dishes and foods that contain tripe. Foods you've most likely eaten. While you may not have had haggis lately, chances are you've eaten a breakfast sausage. How'd that stomach lining taste? What about phở? Menudo? Andouille sausage? Are you able to stomach this information?

At least, as far as the passage of food through the GI tract is concerned, the stomach is above the pyloric sphincter, which, by the way, is also apparently delicious.

You do know that you have a lot of sphincters in your body, right? You even have one in your eye. It's called the pupillary sphincter. It's a little weird to think that you can just walk up to a stranger in public and look deep into his or her sphincter.

Past the pyloric sphincter, things get even weirder in the culinary world. Body parts that are discarded or turned in to fertilizer or fuel here in America are eaten as everyday foods or even delicacies in other parts of the world. One man's sphincter is another man's treasure, as the old adage goes (paraphrase mine). Collectively, the internal organs and entrails of a butchered animal are called *offal.* I believe that this word has the exact same meaning as its most common homophone.

And no, a homophone is not a mobile communications device used by the gay community. You should've paid attention in your high school English class.

Unusual types of offal often comprise traditional holiday dishes. Smalahove is a Norwegian Christmas dish consisting of a dried, salted, boiled sheep's head. Pajata is a dish from Rome consisting of the entrails of a young calf, killed shortly after birth. Head on over to Bavaria for some lung stew, or to Spain for some criadillas, which you might know as Rocky Mountain oysters.

In Romania, you can order khash, which is made from pig feet. Don't pass up a chance to try *sopa de médula,* a soup made from cow brainstem, while in Mexico. And churrasco, consisting of chicken heart, is a must-have in Brazil.

Still hungry? Try the gulai otak (a goat brain curry) or a padang-style deep-fried cow lung in Indonesia. If you can't afford to travel internationally, slurp some bull penis soup in LA or chow a tongue sandwich in NY.

Why would you eat a burger made entirely of cow anus? Ketchup, that's why.

While I commend these efficient usages of every conceivable part of a carcass, these dishes aren't going to tempt me to start eating meat again anytime soon.

I think that in this case our forefathers had it right: offal is best used as a punishment. According to Rictor Norton's essays on gay history and literature: "In 1809 Richard Thomas Dudman and Edward Wood were convicted of a 'conspiracy' to commit sodomy, and sentenced to two years' imprisonment and to stand for one hour in the pillory, where they were pelted with offal supplied by the butchers of Newgate and Fleet Markets."[3]

Sodomy doesn't really seem to be the type of crime that requires a conspiracy to commit. But, what do I know?

It's ironic to me that I live in a country where you can go to jail for kicking someone's cat, even if it has a stupid name like Snowball or Gizmo, yet we can butcher cows and pigs with chainsaws and in other inconceivably inhumane ways. I won't even get into the living conditions these poor animals have to endure. Or the countless health benefits to being vegetarian. Or all the hungry people in the world that could be fed with the gazillions of acres of grain used to fatten up the animals that get turned into a few pounds of meat.

Innumerable studies have shown that vegetarians are healthier and live longer. The results of a 21-year study on almost 2000 people by the German Cancer Research Center show that being a vegetarian cuts your risk of dying young by 41 percent. 41 PERCENT. I'll take it.

Want to save money? Pound for pound, plant protein is three times cheaper than meat protein. Plus, your body is equipped with the enzymes to digest it much more efficiently than meat protein.

Worried about global warming? The Environmental Defense Fund states that every American skipped just *one serving* of meat a week, it would equate to taking *8 million cars* off the road, by reducing the monstrous greenhouse gas emissions from meat production and transport.

Want to reduce your risk of heart attack, cancer, and diabetes? Want to conserve fossil fuels, make antibiotics more effective when you take them, eat more vitamins, avoid obesity, skip the worms and parasites, lower your cholesterol, and lose ten pounds (of rotting flesh in your colon)?

Want to save the lives of 50 animals a year? Try vegetarianism.

How selfish can we be? The average carnivore's response to these arguments is something along the lines of this: "I like meat. I grew up on it. I could never give it up." They might also fumble over some partially made-up statistics about how meat is somehow good for you, and ask how they're supposed to get their protein.

C. David Coats, author of *Old MacDonald's Factory Farm,* puts it poignantly:

"Isn't man an amazing animal? He kills wildlife - birds, kangaroos, deer, all kinds of cats, coyotes, beavers, groundhogs, mice, foxes, and dingoes - by the millions in order to protect his domestic animals and their feed. Then he kills domestic animals by the billions and eats them. This in turn kills man by the millions, because eating all those animals leads to degenerative - and fatal - health conditions like heart disease, kidney disease, and cancer. So then man tortures and kills millions more animals to look for cures for these diseases. Elsewhere, millions of other human beings are being killed by hunger and malnutrition because food they could eat is being used to fatten domestic animals. Meanwhile, some people are dying of sad laughter at the absurdity of man, who kills so easily and so violently, and once a year sends out a card praying for 'Peace on Earth.'"[4]

A scientist once said: "Vegetarian food leaves a deep impression on our nature. If the whole world adopts vegetarianism, it can change the destiny of humankind."

Who was this scientist? Oh, just some dumbass named Albert Einstein.

Turns out, tripe isn't the only meat that's simply offal.

I'D BE PARIS HILTON.

If I had an STD for every time someone hears my name and says, "Oh yeah, you have the same name as the John Davidson that I grew up watching on TV," I'd be Paris Hilton.

Yes, I've heard of him. Yes, though a musician, I'm not primarily a drummer, and thus I possess the brain cells to deduce that even though our first names are an "H" apart, they are essentially the same name. Did I pick my own name? No. Should I adopt a stage name? Since my first choice of pseudonyms, Circling A Rotten Corpse, has already been taken by a band in Iowa, I'm left with a bunch of second-rate options.

Call me what you will. Just don't call me late for dinner.

Every time I heard my grandpa use that stale witticism, I vowed to myself that I'd never follow in his corny footsteps.

If only he could see me now.

I actually prefer his other dinnertime joke, as do three out of four Americans. Following every meal, he'd say, "Glad I ate when I did, 'cause I'm not hungry now."

It's hard to argue with such irrefutable logic.

In any case, I'll stick with the name I've got, thanks. People Of The 70's, I apologize for the confusion.

After all, John Davidson, you're a pretty decent namemate. If this were a contest, a Davidson-off, you would win. You've got *Hollywood Squares* and *That's Incredible!*, and I've got this book. You've got a #7 AC single, and our latest single didn't even chart.

You've been a regular guest host on *The Tonight Show.* I, as you might have guessed, haven't been.

You've posed near-nude for *Cosmo.* I keep on turning such offers down.

However, Mr. John Hamilton Davidson, you're not the only namemate to which I can compare myself. There are other legit individuals out there who share my name, and even spell it correctly.

By 'legit individials,' I mean that they are indeed actually people.

By 'correctly,' I mean that they've wisely and efficiently omitted the H. Just think of the gallons and gallons of ink and toner they've collectively saved over the years. You're welcome, Mother Nature.

There's a congenial-looking gentleman named Jon Davidson who is very concerned with your health, and you can learn more about him and spirulina at jondavidson.com.

There's a gay rights activist who is a lawyer and a director at Lambda Legal, America's largest and oldest legal organization committed to equal civil rights for homosexuals.

There's a doctor of diagnostic radiology at a hospital in Cleveland. A guy who repairs amps in Nashville. An award-winning young hockey player from Florida.

I have also been added as a friend on Facebook by a couple of Jon Davidsons. One Jon Davidson from London actually bought my latest solo album on Amazon and subsequently wrote me to ask if I would be OK with the fact that he is using my album to help him pick up chicks.

We Jon Davidsons are a weird bunch.

Not only do I share a name with some interesting people, but I also share a resemblance. I've been told that I look like everyone from Seann William Scott to Mark McGrath to Willem Dafoe (no thanks).

I used to be nonplussed when strangers would tell me that I look like Matt Damon. This all turned around for me one day a few years ago when, blithely waiting in a checkout line at Safeway, I glanced at the cover of *People*. Matt Damon, it turns out, had just been crowned "Sexiest Man Alive."

On that day, in that inauspicious grocery store, I learned to embrace these comparisons.

WINNING.

Winning.

I don't need a Charlie Sheen meltdown to tell me that it's important.

Vince Lombardi said it best: "Winning isn't everything. It's the only thing."

You don't know who Lombardi is? You are not from Wisconsin, and you probably suck at life.

When teams win the Super Bowl, they get a trophy that is named after him. His name is permanently attached to the award for emerging victorious from the biggest sporting event in the known universe. If that's not winning, I don't know what is.

If you know me, you know that I'm competitive. At everything. I have lost one game of Boggle. In my entire life. To my sister. I'm almost positive she cheated. At least my book is coming out before hers. You can keep your Ph.D, Rahel.

Yes, my sister's name is Rahel. The Hebrew spelling of Rachel, and the contraction of Raw Hell, her WWE moniker.

Life is a competition. We compete for our parents' attention. Then, we compete for attention of the opposite sex. Then, we compete for our boss' attention. Then, we compete for our kids' attention. Then, we die.

Might as well win on your way out.

The beauty of life is that everything can be turned into a competition. You're telling me you've never pulled up to a red light and gunned it off the line to beat the guy in the next lane?

Impromptu drag racing worked out a whole lot better in my Volkswagen GTI VR6 than it did in my first car, a 3-cylinder Geo Metro. One of my three cylinders actually died at one point in 2003, which led to a 20-mph 'ascent' of Monarch Pass in Colorado. On an Interstate. I saw a lot of middle finger that day.

Losing.

I don't buy in to the recent trends in child psychology that stipulate that everyone needs to feel like a winner. If you receive a 9th place ribbon, and you entered a race with ten contestants, how good can you really feel about yourself? What color is a 9th place ribbon, traditionally? I'm assuming some flaccid shade of mauve or chartreuse.

This is why I have a real problem with affirmative action. Sure, I'm all for equality in the workplace. Sure, I recognize that certain ethnic groups have been marginalized in the past, as have certain genders. (Since there are only two known genders, I trust that it's pretty clear that I'm talking about women here.) However, do you really want to get a job, or a scholarship, or an accolade, based on your skin color or gender rather than your accomplishments?

I recognize that quotas have to be filled. But if your house is burning down, and you're trapped inside, who do you want helping you to safety? A muscular 190-lb. man, or a dainty 105-lb. woman? I would prefer to be carried down the stairs, not dragged by my feet.

I'm not insinuating that no women are qualified to be firefighters, and I'd also like to point out that I'm fully aware of the fact that women are superior to men in a multitude of areas, including, but not limited to, the art of Christmas present wrapping. However, it stands to reason that job positions should be filled on the basis of qualification alone, not on the basis of equal rights or a diversified workforce.

Everyone wants to win. But everyone wants to earn it. No one wants to feel like the victory was handed to them. Well, perhaps Antwan Jamison (and every other has-been veteran who signed with the Los Angeles Lakers this year) does. I have spoken too soon.

I want to win. At everything. When I walk into a bathroom and pony up to a urinal next to another guy, you bet I want to start, and finish, peeing before he does, thereby getting to the sink and paper towels first and avoiding any awkward potty talk.

I once entered an impromptu tangerine-eating contest at a house party. I fit six in my mouth simultaneously, and nearly gagged to death. I won, though. Had I died, I at least would have gone out a champion.

Have you ever played Catch Phrase with me? Probably not, if we're still friends. I am not a gracious loser. Nor a gracious winner, for that matter.

My dad used to annihilate me at tennis. At the age of five, I would stand quivering on one side of the court, racket in one hand, pacifier in the other, as my cruel father sent ace after 100-mph ace speeding past my small, underdeveloped hands. So, once I became a teenager, I retaliated by beating him in basketball some 26 games in a row. I also retaliated by never cleaning my room, coming home at 2 AM, and becoming a musician. Vengeance is mine.

I have a hard time with the whole Biblical "first shall be last" train of thought. This defies logic. I'd rather side with Ricky Bobby's dad on this one: "If you ain't first, you're last."

To be fair, even Reese Bobby later acknowledged that he was high the day he said that. "You can be second, third, fourth... hell you can even be fifth."

The apostle Paul put it like this: "Do you not know that in a race all the runners run, but only one gets the prize? Run in such a way as to get the prize. Everyone who competes in the Olympic Games goes into strict training. They do it to get a crown that will not last, but we do it to get a crown that will last forever."

There are a few things in life worth competing for. The best part about this lasting crown is that there isn't just one. Everyone can win. In fact, the crown has already been won for us by the ultimate competitor, the man who sacrificed everything to gain victory. This guy beat out death, pain and sin head-to-head.

If that's not winning, I don't know what is.

SNAKES ON THE YANKEES' PLANE.

I'm in love with a python. Her name is Rose.

There, I said it. I ain't skerred.

She slithers; she sheds her skin like a tube sock; she's the Biblical metaphor for evil. What's not to love? Plus, she's the perfect accessory to many outfits. With scales of tan, black, and brown, it's easy to throw her around your neck for that finishing touch. Where do you think the name 'boa' came from, anyway?

I met Rose while on tour in Boise, ID. She belongs to Geri Lynn, a friend/fan/hairstylist extraordinaire.

I'd never really held a snake before. I think I might have pet one or two at those dumb petting zoos that your parents take you to as a child. You can stick your hand through a hole and pet a goat, but all you really want to do is grab it by the horns and take it for a wild joyride on the icy back roads of Michigan. No? You never wanted to do that? I was a weird kid. A pain in the asp, you might say.

After spending some quality time with Rose, I now know that I need a snake. The only deterrent, for me, is the fact that I would have to feed those poor little hapless mice to it. Not only do I feel bad for the mice, but it's kind of emasculating to tell a snake that a small rodent is the biggest thing it's capable of taking on. Something bigger, albeit dumber, might be more of a challenge.

Something like a sloth. Or a Yankees fan.

I don't actually hate the Yankees. It's not their fault that they have spent their way to the top and plutocratically ruled baseball for the last hundred-plus years. For a little perspective, the Yankees spent about as much on payroll as the Royals, Rays, Padres, Pirates and Indians *combined* this past season. But, if you have the money, why not spend it? It's actually Major League Baseball's fault for failing to impose a hard salary cap.

Money won't buy happiness, but it *will* buy A-Rod, C.C. Sabathia, and Mark Teixeira.

Having said this, I have no problem turning Yankees *fans* into snake feed. If you actually grew up in New York, good for you. You're one of the few who at least root for Satan's team honestly. According to the latest census, the population of New York City is 8,363,710. If all were right with the world, half of NYC would cheer for the Mets, leaving us with exactly 4,181,855 true Yankees fans in existence.

Common sense and jersey sales figures tell me that there are quite a few more than this. I've seen Yankees merchandise sported in practically every state and country I've been to. I'm sure we all know at least one unfortunate person who has been tragically stricken with pinstripe fever. It's easy to root for a team with 27 World Series championships. The Bronx's financial juggernaut has won more World Series than 21 other Major League franchises combined.

The famed historian Josephus indicates that both Caligula and Nero were avid Yankees fans, attending games whenever they weren't busy watching lions devour innocent children.

That's why I smile inside every time I see someone wearing a Pittsburgh Pirates hat. After 19 straight losing seasons, there aren't a whole lot of reasons for jumping on the Pirates' bandwagon. Unless you're tall. There's undoubtedly a lot of room on said bandwagon, so if you're of above-average stature, you'll be comfortably able to stretch your legs.

If I were a screenwriter, my magnum opus would be a sequel to the herpetological Hollywood flop.

I'd call it *Snakes On The Yankees' Plane.* Nobody would die, but who wouldn't want to see A-Rod shooting up with a roided-out anaconda en route to a game?

Truthfully, that wouldn't make very good movie material at all. Might as well write the snakebite-induced death of at least one Yankee fan into the script. That fan might as well be Jack Nicholson.

Why? Well, for starters, he's also a Lakers fan.

And let's not forget who brought us *Man Trouble* and *Something's Gotta Give.*

OF BOMBS AND BLACKBERRIES.

There is nothing worse than a blackberry bush infestation. Nothing.

Okay, so you might be able to make a compelling case for the Holocaust taking over the top spot.

I bought my house five years ago. Little did I know that the quarter-acre lot it's situated on is a fertile breeding ground for this relentless scourge.

The worst part about blackberry bushes is the fact that they bear a delicious fruit. One of my personal favorites.

It's almost as if Osama bin Laden were a world-class oil painter. Don't you think that President Obama, before sending in the commandos that took bin Laden's life, would've had some second thoughts about depriving the world of this modern-day van Gogh if this were indeed the case?

I want to hate blackberry bushes like I hate terrorism. I want them to be the incarnation of pure depravity. Why do blackberries have to taste so good and be so replete with polyphenols?

They are pernicious and delicious.

It's this intermingling of good and evil that angers me the most. Every year, I've paid a landscaping company to rid my backyard of its thorny plague. Every year, the bushes grow back with a vengeance, and every year I enjoy some delicious, antioxidant-laden blackberries. Every year, I agonize over the decision to once again destroy these virulent plants, but can rest assured that any herbicide or removal method thrown at them will ultimately prove impotent and unable to curb their growth onslaught.

I wish that life were more cut-and-dry.

Take terrorism, for instance.

Of course, 9/11 was an atrocity. Of course, the shooting at Ft. Hood was barbaric. Of course, the attacks on Mumbai, London, and the like were equally heinous acts of malevolent cowardice. Simply searching for 'terrorist incidents' on Wikipedia brings up a horror-filled list of literally hundreds of terrorist acts that span the globe. And that's just for this last year alone.

However, one can easily look at the other side of the coin: the inconspicuous imperialism of America is a slippery eel. The evidence is hard to ignore: we've taken sides in the Middle East for decades, and have carefully tried to manipulate scores of governments and regimes for our own benefit. We've killed thousands of innocent civilians in Afghanistan, Iraq and elsewhere across the region in the process. We've turned a blind eye and provided financial aid to Israel while they've killed Palestinian civilians at an alarming rate.

Don't misinterpret this: terrorism is absolutely wrong and evil, and is by no means the correct response to our decades of meddling in the Middle East. It's the equivalent of the fourth grader who, after years of being bullied by a bigger classmate, shows up to school one day with a knife and stabs him to death. Was he provoked? Yes. Were his actions justified? Absolutely not.

More importantly, I'm still left with the problem of what to do about the pestilence in my backyard.

Did you know that blackberry bushes are not indigenous to the Pacific Northwest? European explorers brought *R. lacinatus* to Oregon in 1850. I want to exhume the bodies of these explorers and punch them in the medulla oblongata, or perhaps track down their descendants and present them with a bill for the landscaping I've paid for over the past few years.

It's fair to say these explorers left their mark: Oregon is now the world's #1 producer of blackberries.

Folklore in Great Britain holds that blackberries should not be picked after Old Michaelmas Day, as the devil has claimed them, having left his mark on the leaves by urinating on them.

Old Michaelmas Day falls on October 11, of course. But you knew that.

It's great to know that we live in a world where Satan has nothing better to do than to go around and pee on plants. In light of hundreds of terrorist attacks during this past year alone, we've apparently taken care of all the depravity that this world can handle on our own, leaving the devil with a lot of time on his hands.

I just wish that El Diablo could get his act together and pee on my blackberries a little earlier this year, killing the plants and thereby saving me the trouble and indignity of exhuming a bunch of graves.

DITTY NECTAR.

I used to have time to write music regularly.

About as regularly as Lindsay Lohan getting a DUI, cocaine being found in Lindsay Lohan's car, Lindsay Lohan going to rehab, Lindsay Lohan going to the hospital, et al..

Now, it seems that finding the time to write songs happens as infrequently as Lindsay Lohan appearing in a good movie, or Lindsay Lohan just generally making a good decision of any kind.

Why am I picking on Ms. Lohan? I don't know. This ginger nut job (GNJ) is old news. Forgive me for not having the time to keep up on the latest brainless she-tabloid fodder.

By the way, I'd like to thank Ms. White, my junior high English teacher, for cementing in my brain the basic rules of grammar and syntax that have paved the way for me to feebly undertake lyrical authorship. I would also like to thank her for somewhat creepily telling me that I should wear pleated khakis every day because I looked so good in them. For the record, it is mathematically impossible to look good in pleated khakis. Then again, Ms. White didn't teach math.

It seems that the more your career progresses, the less time you have to actually focus on the music, which is in theory what said career is all about. Furthermore, when it comes to writing music, there's no one looking over your shoulder, no one to keep you on track but yourself.

Plus, it's really hard to write while in a van with three other unshaven dudes. I prefer the solace of a quiet room. Perhaps I'm being too picky.

In 2010, for instance, Crown Point toured to Houston and back in March, and Illinois and back in July, playing at SxSW and Cornerstone Festival and breaking down eight times along the way. In August, we recorded an album in Vancouver, BC with Jeff Johnson, a producer with an affinity for zipper masks (don't ask) who has worked with the likes of Nickelback, Jet Black Stare, and Adelitas Way. Nickelback's drummer, Daniel Adair, played drums on one song on the album, much to the chagrin of rock purists and the joy of popheads who are smiling everywhere.

How can you not smile, albeit mainly condescendingly, at a band that writes lyrics like "What the hell is on Joey's head?"

In any case, Nickelback is smiling all the way to the bank.

Did you know that in Pocatello, Idaho, the self-proclaimed Smile Capital of the US, you can be issued a ticket for frowning in public? Look it up. It seems like a vicious cycle to me: you're issued a ticket, causing you to frown even more. At this point, you're issued another ticket, and so on. But, who am I to judge the means by which a city generates revenue? Unless it's child prostitution, of course. At that point, I could probably feel good about judging.

We commuted back and forth to Vancouver, BC the entire month of August so as to avoid canceling any shows. If Chester's Chicken can feature a smiling cowboy chicken in its logo, who is undoubtedly a) thrilled about the fact that he's about to be cruelly slaughtered and eaten and b) a diehard country music fan, I can call it a commute, okay?

After a couple of weekend tours to eastern Idaho, we then headed to Alaska for two shows at the Alaska State Fair, sharing the lineup with Shinedown and Collective Soul, and took a couple days off to visit Denali and consume an entire hippo-sized gourd.

I then spent two days in Portland before flying to the Philippines to produce an album for an artist from Guam.

Then, after another two days in Portland, Crown Point and I embarked on a 2-month nationwide tour, opening for Tyrone Wells and Andrew Belle. If you haven't checked out Tyrone and Andrew, do yourself a favor, get cozy in your limited-edition Weezer Snuggie, and listen to their music. Tyrone is best known for a couple of Top-20 hits, including "More." If his music doesn't make you think about what really matters, then you most likely don't understand English, which makes the fact that you're managing to read this dramatically undermine your credibility.

On our fall 2010 tour, we hit Boise, Idaho Falls, Denver, Cheyenne, Oklahoma City, Dallas, Austin, Houston, Birmingham, Atlanta, Nashville, DC, Annapolis, New York, Philly, Boston, Wilmington, South Bend, Chicago, Indy, St. Louis, Minneapolis, Milwaukee, Iowa City, Lawrence, Colorado Springs, Salt Lake, Provo, Spokane, San Luis Obispo, San Diego, LA, Sacramento, San Francisco, Portland, and Seattle. To name a few.

Between the beginning of July 2010 and the end of November 2010, I was home in Portland for a grand total of six whole days.

In 2011, we took it easy, by comparison. We only played 168 shows and toured in a mere 24 states. In 2012, we're touring the US, Canada, and Australia.

Life never slows down. In fact, it's just the opposite.

I need to find a way to squeeze writing into my agenda. Perhaps I should start sleeping with a guitar in my hands and a video camera running. Who knows? The recording might capture proof that I am the world's first somnambulating songwriter. More likely, though, it would capture proof that I just rolled over in my sleep and crushed yet another thousand-dollar instrument.

I think I see the flaw in my plan.

In any case, I need to find the time to get the ditty nectar flowing again.

Think of all the time I could have saved in hard returns had I simply used standard paragraph indent formatting instead of placing a double space in between each paragraph in an attempt to make this book seem sui generis. And the period after each chapter title? Each represents another frivolous moment wasted in the pursuit of layout vanity. At least I saved a lot of time on this book's wretched table of contents, and by getting most of my facts from Wikipedia.

Maybe I just need to stop spending so much time pretending I'm an author.

TWELVE OR OH-TWELVE.

Happy New Year. Or something.

Isn't New Year's kind of ridiculous? First of all, there are way too many different calendars in use, each with their own New Year's date. There's the Gregorian calendar, the Chinese or Xia calendar, the Swimsuit calendar..

Who was this Gregorian guy, anyway? And why should he dictate the one night that most Americans decide to get wasted?

Actually, that's pretty much every night. What country besides the USA celebrates *other* countries' independence days simply in order to find another excuse to drink?

Did you know that Cinco de Mayo (which is not even Mexico's official independence day) is only officially celebrated in one Mexican state?

Did you know that Mexico has states?

Back to Gregory: apparently, he was a pope. He was the eighth pope named Gregory. In those days, all you had to do if you wanted your son to become Pope was to name him Gregory. Oh yeah, and make sure he was white, and lived in Rome. And looked good in a mitre.

Letting him die of the Black Plague would probably diminish his chances of ascending to the papacy, as well, so keeping your son in good health was a must.

I digress.

Anyway, Gregory XIII introduced his namesake calendar in 1582 by way of papal bull. This holy cow spread the word regarding the new calendar, goring and trampling those who dared not to adopt it. Regardless of what Wikipedia says, a papal bull is *not* another word for a pontiff's decree. It's a very angry animal that will literally rip your heathen face off.

Gregory's calendar replaced that of Julius Caesar. Rather than feel disenfranchised, Julius quickly realized that his future was in the orange fruit smoothie business, and the rest is history.

With Gregorian New Years come New Year's Resolutions. They suck. What makes otherwise sane individuals think that they'll somehow be imbued with all the self-control that they couldn't muster the year before? I wonder how long the average New Year's resolution lasts. Probably not even as long as Kevin Federline's career.

Why do we as humans lack self-discipline? I speak for myself here: I'm brimming with good intentions, yet my actions and choices consistently fall short of the mark that my heart and mind have set. Paul, the famous Biblical author, put it this way: "For what I want to do I do not do."

New Year's seems to be just another quick-fix solution, another South Beach Diet, another HydroxyCut. In reality, it's just another day: according to the Julian calendar, January 1 is actually December 21, so clearly the day itself has no overarching importance.

As P.O.D. put it, "Every day is a new day...so I learn from my mistakes." (When was the last time that a reputable author began a sentence with “as P.O.D. put it”? Never, that’s when.)

That's the key, I think: not trying to flip a switch. We can't become totally different people overnight; change and growth take time. If we continuously learn from our shortcomings and learn to love just a little bit better, we'll accomplish in time what a thousand different well-intentioned New Year's Resolutions never could.

One last question of utmost importance has been weighing on my mind. Should we refer to 2012 as 'Twelve' or 'Oh-Twelve'?

I’ve faced this dilemma in tortured silence for the past three years. Obviously, 2009 was 'Oh-Nine.' So it would seem logical that we would continue to use the last two digits of the year to refer to the year shorthandedly. 'Twelve,' though, just doesn't flow. It seems more appropriate when used in reference to my pant size in women's jeans. Don't judge me.

However, although 'Oh-Twelve' is still technically equitable, it just doesn't make sense. Nobody says 'Oh-Oh-Nine'. Unless they stutter. If Gandhi were alive right now, my first, and arguably only, important question to him would be: "How did you abbreviate 1912?" I'm sure that he would non-violently resist the use of any inferior abbreviations.

I guess we'll never know.

MWAHAHAHAHAHAHA.

Just your average cachinnatory onomatopœia.

In other words, the title of this chapter is the transliteration of my evil laugh as I fly to the Philippines to produce an album and assume creative control of someone else's musical aspirations.

This sadistic desire dates from the days of 'group learning' projects in high school where, much to the delight of the rest of my group, I would often complete the entire assignment myself to make sure it was done, and done right.

I also take charge of my wardrobe. I iron my own shirts, but I don't fold my underwear. Nobody folds my underwear. I pity the fool.

I also like to dominate grapes. I love popping the hapless fruits between my lips so that they snap back against the roof of my mouth, sometimes two or three at a time. In grape-tossing situations, I also prefer to be the 'pitcher', not the 'catcher', despite the large size of my mouth.

It was this desire to call the shots and exercise creative control, while in the studio with my hard rock band Silversafe, that initially led me to record (and produce) my first solo album, and embark on my career as a solo artist. While working on Crown Point's new album, it was this same desire that caused our producer, Jeff Johnson, to want to pat me on the back at times. By 'pat', I mean 'slap', and by 'back' I mean 'face', of course.

Now, I've been hired to produce an album overseas. The artist? Cara, a singer/songwriter from Guam. As a result, I find myself sitting in seat 29G on Korean Air Flight 20, headed for Seoul and ultimately Manila.

The best part about being on an airplane is knowing that you're safe. From earthquakes.

I have one word for you. That word, of course, is Gochujang.

Never heard of it? You will. It's the nubile Korean hot pepper paste that, for an afternoon at 35,000 feet, made my mouth very, very happy, salvaging an otherwise prison-worthy meal of rice, seaweed soup, some chili pickle concoction, and of course honeydew.

To be honest, Gochujang and honeydew were meant for each other. It was a beautiful thing. Brought tears to my eyes, tears which had much to do with the fact that I emptied the rest of the 20-gram tube on the hapless honeydew before inserting the whole mess in my mouth amid the polite giggles of my seatmate.

I laughed, too.

Little does she know that I only cracked up because she smells like baby powder. Did she just have her diaper changed? I have no idea.

Two thumbs up for Korean Air and their extraordinary hospitality, by the way. If I had been blessed with a third thumb, it would be up as well. Honestly the most courteous and helpful flight attendants I've ever seen.

In any case, I'm looking forward to producing this record, and looking forward to finding a way to sneak the words "orphan meat" into every single song.

Who knows? This could be the start of an unexpected career path for me. Long after I've passed the age of commercial viability as an artist, and long after my face has been repeatedly steam-pressed by the ubiquitous Brotox iron, I could still be lending my creative input to young artists who are thankfully too young to remember and remind me of the 'other' John Davidson, not to mention the landmark embarrassments of my time: New Coke, Darfur, George W., and, of course, Three Doors Down.

There's an ad in the Korean Air in-flight magazine that declares: "2010-2012: Visit Korea Year."

Here's hoping that these next three years will be one amazing year.

I've slept for four hours in the last 40, and delirium is starting to kick in. We're starting to descend into Seoul, and it's a gloomy day. I was just informed over the loudspeaker that it's 25 degrees Celsius on the ground, which, I'm told, is equivalent to 55 degrees Fahrenheit. Hmm…probably just the exchange rate.

I've got a two-hour layover in Seoul, and a four-hour flight to Manila, followed by an hour taxi ride to Makati City.

Annyonghi kasayo.

HERE'S A TIP, OPRAH.

By now, if you're in the service industry, you've likely heard about Oprah's recession-busting advice.

No, it has nothing to do with wise investment, or passing on that 52" plasma. Or cooking up your own crack rather than going out and buying that high-grade coke.

Her advice? It's simple. Don't tip.

Continue to go out to eat as often as you'd like, and spend as much as you'd like. But tipping? So 2007.

When in doubt, ask yourself: what would Oprah tip? WWOT?

Never mind that servers in many states make well below minimum wage from their employers. Somewhere around $2.13 an hour, last I checked. Never mind that servers are taxed by the IRS on their total sales, whether they make tips on those sales or not. Never mind that servers must also tip out bartenders and hosts, and sometimes bussers and cooks, out of what they make on a given evening.

Never mind that if the US decided to legislate a mandated minimum wage for the service industry, restaurants would be forced to raise food and beverage prices dramatically to compensate for all the additional payroll costs.

I think it's great that someone has finally spoken up and said "enough is enough." Service industry personnel should make less money, and Oprah should make more. Nothing does one's heart more good than to take money from the working poor simply because Oprah said so.

It's almost the holiday season! Homeless servers can still have Christmas trees; they just have to leave them where they found them, in the city park. Oh, and they can't decorate them, either. Presents? Well, finding that half-eaten donut in the trash is kind of like a present from a stranger. Wrap it up in Big Mac paper, and you've got yourself a regular Christmas!

What's that? You celebrate Hanukkah? You're going to have a harder time finding latkes, those traditional potato pancakes, in the dumpster. Would cold french fries that have been soggily pressed together count?

Look what you've done, Oprah.

There was a time when Oprah worked for a living. A time when she brushed her own teeth, wiped her own butt.

Now, there are people for that.

That's why her advice, to me, seems so paradoxical. Once upon a time, Oprah was pregnant at age 14. Once upon a time, Oprah was a local news co-anchor in Baltimore. Once upon a time, her last name was Winfrey. Oprah singlehandedly created the overarching media empire she presides over today. It seems that owning private jets, hosting the highest-rated show in history, and gracing the cover of your eponymous magazine every month has a way of smashing those early memories into a Million Little Pieces.

I've heard it said: Every time you don't tip, God kills a kitten. Oprah *hates* kittens. When was the last time you saw one on the cover of her magazine?

She also hates residing in only one place. Oprah owns at least nine houses, including a 42-acre oceanview estate in California, purchased solely with all the money she's saved on gratuity over the years.

It's so simple! Don't tip. Buy mansions. Gain 400 pounds.

Let me clarify two things: First, this chapter is not meant to be an exercise in Oprah-bashing. While her statement on tipping showed incredible ignorance and callousness, she has done a lot of philanthropic good with the wealth she has amassed. Oprah's Angel Network has raised over $51 million for underprivileged individuals. She personally donates more of her own money to charity than any other show-business celebrity in America. This is a fact.

Second, I'm not suggesting that you tip 30 percent across the board whether you felt you were adequately serviced or not. Without getting into specific numbers and percentages, though, I do believe that a good tip is always appropriate, unless the server gave you herpes or a comparable disease during the course of dinner.

Listen to Oprah. She has a lot of good things to say.

But ignore, if you will, her advice on tipping. Not to mention her advice on weight loss.

People in the service industry work hard for a living, and few outside of the industry really understand the ins and outs of sub-$3 hourly wages, tipping out, and overtaxation. Servers and bartenders survive on tips. Just the tip. Just for a second...just to see how it feels.

Here's a tip, Oprah: I'd advise you to stay silent on issues you don't fully understand.

Of Bombs And Blackberries is evidence that this is a piece of advice that I clearly don't follow myself, but no matter. Do as I say, not as I do.

Furthermore, I wouldn't eat out for a while, unless you genuinely enjoy the taste of other people's spit.

I trust that your seventeen live-in chefs get rather bored when you go out to eat, anyway.

THE RUBIK'S CUBE THAT COULD CHANGE THE WORLD.

You'd think it was my first time on an airplane.

I failed to bring any reading material whatsoever with me on my flight home from Vancouver, BC. The copy of the Horizon Airlines magazine in the seat in front of me has a soggy, crumb-filled bottom.

Not unlike my great aunt Betty.

I'm sitting in seat 8D, directly adjacent to the right wing's propeller. Those things are louder than a baby getting circumcised, which could actually be happening somewhere else on the plane for all I know. Fortunately, the props are blocking out the sound of the greasy chick's iPod from across the aisle. The screen says she's rocking out to some Gaga.

The 8-year old kid sitting next to me just finished a Rubik's Cube competition in Vancouver. He got a nineteen-second solve time on a regular cube, and I just watched him demonstrate his ability solve a 5x5 cube in about three minutes. Pretty amazing. As you might guess, he sports a pocket protector, is a total dork, will die a virgin, and will probably end up making some incredible technological or scientific discovery that will change the world.

Ah, Horizon Airlines. Free Jones Soda and Oktoberfest. Why must your flights be so short?

On my flight up to BC yesterday, I sat next to James Curleigh, the former CEO of Salomon Sporting Goods and the current president of Portland-based Keen Footwear. He's a super chill guy, and a closet musician himself. He invited me up to his brother's downtown penthouse last night to hang with the guys from Our Lady Peace, but unfortunately we were mixing our album in the studio until after 1 am.

I also almost got invited to party with Taylor Swift. Unfortunately, Kanye ran up and grabbed her phone right as she was about to give me a call.

What is it about the spotlight that people crave? Attention is a good thing; everyone wants to be noticed, and everyone wants to be valued. These are basic human traits that we all share.

Not all of us are cut out to be the Voice Of Our Generation.

What is it about celebrities that makes our culture hold their every word, their every viewpoint, in such high regard?

The top story on Yahoo.com recently was the fact that Paris Hilton's wisdom has been immortalized in the renowned Oxford Book Of Quotations. Her quote? "Dress cute wherever you go, life is too short to blend in."

Don't think for a minute, though, that Paris doesn't know what it's like to suffer, much like the victims of 9/11. In the words of her mega-hit "Jailhouse Baby," there's a crazy world at war, right outside of her front door...like a public enemy...all those lonely nights of terror...

What did Paris have to say about being featured in such a

distinguished book alongside the likes of Confucius, Martin Luther King Jr., and Stephen Hawking? "So cool that I have a quote in the dictionary," she wrote. ZOMG, girl, that is, like, so cool, LMFAO!

What's next? Paris for President? At the Palms chilling with a martini. Paris For President. Your commander in bikini!

Fittingly, Oxford opted to print her epic quotation with incorrect punctuation. You guessed it: that should be a semicolon, not a comma, in between clauses.

Why do we as a culture care so much about what pop icons do and say, even pop icons who have reduced themselves to laughingstocks, much like Kanye and Paris? Why do we care so little about people who are doing things that really matter? If it isn't entertainment-related, it gets filtered directly into the Spam folder of our brains.

Someone once auctioned off Paris Hilton's boarding pass from a flight to Fiji for $205.00. What is that lucky buyer going to do with it? Pay their mortgage? Feed their kids? "Put a little more ketchup on it, little Jimmy. No dessert till you're finished!"

Have you heard of Daniel Nocera? Me neither. He's the MIT chemist at the forefront of developing a new method for making hydrogen fuel from water. Within a few years, we could be meeting global energy needs from a few smaller bodies of water.

What about Somaly Mam? She's a Cambodian who escaped from a horrific decade of sexual slavery and torture in a brothel in Phnom Penh. She has started a nonprofit organization that works with police to raid brothels and liberate women from a terrible and unspeakable existence. She has already helped more than 4,000 women escape and find their lives again. She's had to endure the kidnap and rape of her own 14-year old daughter by brothel owners bent on deterring her work.

I'd like to give TIME Magazine mad dope super-fly props for their issues featuring the 100 most influential people in the world. Rather than filling the pages with Paris and Kanye, they've brought to light the stories of people around the globe who are doing things that truly matter, things that make a tangible difference in the lives of real people.

Think those 4,000 former sex slaves would find the words to Kanye's "Therapy" or Paris' "Human Sacrifice" touching?

You know a celebrity or two. You know a hero. That teacher who inspired you to learn. That parent who loves you unconditionally no matter how many times you screamed and slammed your door growing up. That friend who brought you over that mint chocolate chip ice cream when the love of your life broke your heart and let you cry all the tears that you had. People doing things to better our environment, our society, our health, our souls.

Maybe we should listen to what *these* people have to say.

APOLOGETICS. APOLOGETICALLY.

I'm a Christian.

I hesitate to use the term in some circles, because it immediately conjures up images of Rick Santorum gay-bashing and ultimately getting an Urban Dictionary term named after him. Look it up.

I wish Rick would take the term 'gay-bashing' literally and bash a homosexual or two. With a pan or something. Not because I want anyone to get hurt, but because then Santorum would be arrested and locked away, finally putting an end to his nonsense and his political career.

I'm pretty sure Jesus himself has had a laugh or two at Santorum's expense.

I have a few reasons for what I believe. Appropriately, the branch of theology dealing with a defense or proof of Christianity is called apologetics. This, I believe, is because Christianity has to do a lot of apologizing for its Christians. Christians who hate, judge, even kill people in the name of God.

However, individuals such as Stalin killed tens of millions in the name of atheism, so don't blame religion for everything. You can, however, solely blame religion for Glenn Beck, whose birth was the third-worst event of 1964, according to a recent poll whose existence and results I completely fabricated.

I'm a Christian because it's the only religion which fundamentally centers around a deity doing something for us, not the other way around. If you're anything like me, God would seem a lot further off if I had to be really, really good to earn his approval; if I had to achieve some kind of moral credit score in order to be approved for a loan of grace.

Watch the news. It's hard to buy into the theory that humanity is fundamentally good. When a 1-year-old gets shot and killed during the making of a rap video, we have a problem.

I'm a Christian because when I Tebow (an act formerly known as kneeling to pray), I pray to a God who has already given everything. No rituals necessary. No money needed to buy my way out of purgatory. Not even flawless church attendance or being Mother Teresa II or will get me any closer to where I want to be.

I'm a Christian because the odds of everything in the universe working out the way it has by chance are so slim that they cannot even be estimated, even according to atheist scientists. Somehow, our planet came to be, life spontaneously originated, crawled out of primordial soup, and then somehow turned into the millions of extremely complex trillion-celled organisms alive today. And it's somehow supposed to be hard to believe in God, yet somehow easy to believe in Dawkins' postulated multiverse theory, for which evidence is extremely hard to come by.

However, I hate several things about being a Christian in a predominantly Christian nation. First, I hate the American Christians that think that they are constantly being persecuted for their faith. Shut up and move to Iran and let me know how being a Christian there works out for you.

Second, I hate the fact that a few bad apples have spoiled the bunch. Even though the majority (78 percent) of the US identifies itself as Christian, there's an underlying sense in society that anyone who is a 'real' Christian hates homosexuals, is out to 'witness' to everyone, is blind to scientific progress, and has at least 30 ignorant and intolerant bumper stickers per bumper. Guess what? The Jesus of the Bible was out to distance himself and his message of grace from these types of 'religious' people too. Yeah, that same party animal Jesus that turned water into mighty fine wine at a wedding.

If Jesus had not been the Son of God with a few more important agenda items to accomplish, a bartending gig would've worked out really well for him. Imagine how many regulars he would've accrued. I for one would definitely drive out of my way to order a few glasses of water so I could sit back and watch what happened next.

Plus, water is on the house. Wine is not. I'm not making millions off of book and album sales here.

Anyway, back to my hate countdown.

Third, what happened to the separation of church and state? I'm tired of all this 'let's get back to the faith of our founding fathers' drivel. We don't need laws and constitutions to protect us from all these so-called evils and the decadence of our modern society. Sure, things have gotten worse in some aspects. But, they've also gotten better. Today, we don't generally watch people get fed to lions for sport on Sunday afternoons. (Only on Thursdays.) Say what you will, all you little old ladies, about the violence on TV, but I'll take it over watching jungle cats eat a hominid lunch. Shut up, whiners. If your faith matters and is real, it can exist and thrive in any environment.

Fourth, I hate televangelists. Sixteen luxury cars? More than enough, if you ask me. Sixteen affairs? Same answer. I'm sick of megachurches with their own ZIP code. Read the book of Acts. This is pretty far from what Jesus had in mind.

Fifth, I'm tired of Christians' attempts to needlessly complicate Christianity, turning off millions in the process. Sure, God lays down some rules in the Bible. But Jesus summed it up pretty simply: "Love God, love people. This is what matters most."

Religion says "do." Grace says "done."

Why is this simple and life-changing concept so difficult for most Christians, myself included, to grasp?

Fortunately, I'm not a Christian because of other Christians. I'm a Christian because it's the only logical response to what I know and what I've seen in the short time I've been alive. And I'm definitely not making the claim that I have everything figured out.

André Gide said it best: "Believe those who are seeking the truth. Doubt those who find it."

Literally thousands of books have been written by intelligent Christians defending the reasons for Christianity. Thousands of books have been written by intelligent atheists defending the reasons for godlessness. Every other religion, with the possible exception of the Church Of The Flying Spaghetti Monster, has its countless defenders and detractors. I'm not here to recap what all these treatises have said.

Treatise is kind of a creepy-sounding word. Right up there with ointment and uvula. Or, alternatively, it could be some kind of special gift turtle.

I know that lots of people have a problem with all the pain and suffering in the world. I do too. How can God be good and all-powerful, and still allow it? Well, read the book of Job. We screwed up God's original plan. Since then, God can't just bless the people who love him and everyone else. He wants us to love him, not view him as some sort of celestial Santa Claus who waits to give us toys until we've made the 'nice' list.

In his eye-opening book, *Jesus Mean And Wild,* Mark Galli writes: "Perhaps the greatest danger—and the most tempting idol—is to imagine that God is the servant of our desires, who meets all our needs and is there for us in crises in exactly the way we need him to be there for us. But this idol is built on a false base, as if our desires are the measure of what is best for us, as if our "needs" are really our deepest needs, as if the only and best way to resolve a crisis is to do so in the way we think it should be resolved—as if we were all-wise, all-knowing, and all-loving."[5]

Plus, it's not like Jesus lived some semi-charmed kind of life, baby. Last I checked, he was born in a barn, worked hard, starved in the desert, walked everywhere, hung out with a bunch of whores and terminally ill people, got betrayed by the people he loved, and was executed in an excruciatingly painful manner in public while being mocked from all sides.

God didn't intervene and make things better for his own Son. Instead, he gave him the punishment we deserve. Why? So that one day he could personally wipe all our tears away for good in a place where death and pain are no more.

So yeah, I'm a Christian. Yeah, I'm tired of other Christians. Yeah, I swear when I pray sometimes. Yeah, I respect people whose beliefs are absolutely nothing like mine. Yeah, I screw up a lot and hurt people. Yeah, God himself is desperately in love with me. Pretty crazy thought.

Is it weird that a Lady Antebellum song makes me cry every time I hear it? "All the empty disappears. I remember why I'm here, to surrender and believe, I fall down on my knees. Hello world."

SPELLBOUND.

Why is it that I can't go to a single restaurant, or brothel for that matter, without finding some kind of spelling error on the menu?

Tonight, at a fine establishment in Atlanta, GA, I was pleased to find a "Pomagranite Martini" for only $7. Yup, it's made with real bits of igneous rocks, so you know it's good.

A title in a brochure published by the University Of Maryland Baltimore County screams: “Perparing your child for college: It’s not too soon.”

The road outside Northwood Elementary in Kalamazoo, MI, just 40 minutes from where I grew up, was painted “SHCOOL” in 2007.

A recent Associated Press headline reads: “Missippi’s Literary Program Shows Improvement.”

There's a well-known and well-liked acoustic music venue in Portland named The Guffalo Bap (names have been changed to protect the ignorant) bearing a sign on its wall that reads "LIVE MUISIC."

The inabbillity too spel is weidspred. But say 'nay' to the naysayers who would have you believe that it's a phenomenon being propagated by texting and pop culture.

It has long been a scourge blighting our country, right up there with poverty, war, and Texas.

Even the venerable U.S. Constitution contains a few misspelled words. Pennsylvania, for instance, is spelled Pensylvania. You can't just take n's out of words arbitrarily and expect to be viewed as a credible source. I don't want to live in Orego. Sounds like a milquetoast herb. Would you listen to my music if my name were Jo? What if the second track on my latest solo album were called "It Won't Be Log"? What does that even mean? Is it a prediction of loose stool?

Of course, not everyone is a great speller. That's why God created spell-checking software. If you can't spell, no problem. Use a machine that is smarter than you. Even Bill Gates himself is famously quoted as saying: "I'm a terrible speller. Fortunately, my good looks have gotten me everywhere."

(Bill Gates never actually said this.)

It's interesting to live in a society where the average schmuck can't spell 'intelligence', but can spell 'Kardashian'.

By the way, do you know what 'schmuck' means in Yiddish? Google it.

Just for the record, I don't judge people for misspelled words in text messages, considering the message was probably sent while driving, going to the bathroom, and reading my book simultaneously. But when I read a book or blog or magazine that's riddled with mistakes, it tends to lose credibility in my mind. Kind of like when former Vice Presidents insist that torturing people is a good idea. (Yeah, I had to slip at least one political line in this otherwise inane chapter somewhere.)

I think the real problem lies in the name 'spelling bee.' Kids quickly associate these with a cute, fuzzy, yellow-and-black insect. Think Honey Nut Cheerios. Childish. Impotent. Thus, kids lose interest. Why not the 'spelling wasp' or even the 'spelling pterodactyl'? Faster. Edgier. More dangerous.

Until we as a society band together and change the name of this ubiquitous competition, letters everywhere will remain captive in incorrect order, and we will remain spellbound.

GET A LIFE, AMERICA.

Cancer is a capricious killer.

It holds no regard for age, gender, race, or geographical location. Practically everyone I know has had a loved one who has died of cancer.

My uncle Bob passed away a couple years ago from malignant melanoma that metastasized.

Another uncle of mine was recently diagnosed with skin cancer. My grandma is a brain tumor survivor. My sister has already had a cancerous lesion removed from her foot.

I've had precancerous moles removed from my back.

Sure, we eat our antioxidants, we wear our sunblock, we quit smoking, and we even stop re-using plastic bottles, in the hopes that we don't become a statistic. But is that all that we can do?

Last year, there were 21,370 new cancer cases reported in Oregon alone, and 7,450 people in Oregon died of cancer. In the US, 565,000 people died from cancer last year. To put this number in perspective, that's just a few thousand less than the population of cities like Portland, Seattle, Nashville, Denver, and Las Vegas. 565,000 is an astonishing figure.

Let's say Portland gets wiped out this year. Whether through a terrorist attack, through a natural disaster, an anti-hipster revolt, or through some other means, the entire population of America's 29th largest city is destroyed.

Think that would make the news?

However, cancer is almost taken for granted. It flies under the radar, a killer to be sure, but one that's accepted as a tragic mainstay of society. We're all immortal until it's our turn.

It's time to do something. Not just for ourselves, but for society as a whole.

The American Cancer Society, among other organizations, has been fighting the good fight for years. I love this quote on their website:

"Eleven million cancer survivors will celebrate birthdays this year. That's a sign of progress, proof that a world with more birthdays is possible. Together we'll get well, stay well, find cures, and fight back."

Here's the deal: let's say you're a man. Like me. I'm not saying that you're like me in any way, or that you'll ever be as much of a man as I already was at age 6. I'm strictly referring to your chromosomes. Well, sir, your odds of developing cancer at some point in your life are 1 in just over 2. Of course, many cancers are genetic or caused by a variety of immutable factors. However, let's take a good look in the mirror and realize that a large number of cancer cases are our own fault. According to cancer.org:

"All cancers caused by cigarette smoking and heavy use of alcohol could be prevented completely. The American Cancer Society estimates that in 2012 about 173,200 cancer deaths will be caused by tobacco use. Scientific evidence suggests that about one-third of the 577,190 cancer deaths expected to occur in 2012 will be related to overweight or obesity, physical inactivity, and poor nutrition and thus could also be prevented. Certain cancers are related to infectious agents, such as hepatitis B virus (HBV), human papillomavirus (HPV), human immunodeficiency virus (HIV), Helicobacter pylori (H. pylori), and others, and could be prevented through behavioral changes, vaccines, or antibiotics. In addition, many of the more than 2 million skin cancers that are diagnosed annually could be prevented by protecting skin from intense sun exposure and avoiding indoor tanning."

If we as a nation quit smoking, stopped drinking so much, exercised more, ate more healthfully, stopped having unprotected sex, and wore sunblock, somewhere around 480,000 fewer Americans would die from cancer this year alone.

Holy cow.

Remember the Iraq War? That conflict that most Americans, myself included, saw as fruitless after taking the towering death toll into consideration? Anywhere from 100,000 to 150,000 civilians and combatants are estimated to have died from this entirely preventable war. Tragic, senseless, and horrific, to be sure. But, think of it this way: approximately *four times* as many people die from entirely preventable cancers. In America. Every single year.

You don't see many hippies up in arms about *this.*

420,000 people live in Atlanta. What if you could save their lives heroically every year? Or, what if they had the power to save their own lives every year, but opted instead for one more cigarette, one more cheeseburger, and one more shot?

"Preventative medicine? What in tarnation is that? Is that like wearing two condoms and taking a Vicodin at the same time? I reckon."

Get a life, America.

I've been guilty of engaging in carcinogenic activities myself. I've never smoked or lined up straight shots of formaldehyde (yes, both of these substances have approximately the same effect on your overall health), but I've done my fair share of tanning, and until recently have eaten a preservative-heavy diet. However, I've done my best to quit these harmful behaviors and to be healthy on a daily basis. I've been privileged to play at numerous American Cancer Society fundraiser events over the past few years, and dedicated each performance to my uncle Bob.

We have all felt cancer's icy touch, whether upon ourselves or someone we love. It's high time we do something about it. We need to donate to research. Volunteer our time. Bring encouragement to a cancer patient.

Even more indubitably, we need to get healthy and take control of the odds.

We can't wait around for someone else to make a difference.

FRUITCAKE MERRILY ON HIGH.

When did Christmas get all prima donna and demand its own month?

Every other holiday gets merely a single day. In 1492, Columbus sailed the ocean blue, but he doesn't even get more than 24 hours and a lame excuse for financial institutions to take the day off? Do you know how hard it was to sail around the earth back when it was flat? This is how we say thanks?

Sure, some of the more prestigious holidays might command a weekend. Halloween stores do open up a couple weeks before October 31, and Irish people find reasons to get drunk year-round, not just on March 17. But, Christmas is still in a class all its own.

Sadly, Yuletide's length enshrouds some other meaningful December holidays in its bloated wreath-shaped shadow. Holidays like Forefathers' Day, December 21, which shouldn't be confused with Four Fathers Day, a celebration of homosexual plural marriage. Holidays like Pepper Pot Day, December 29. And, of course, my personal favorite, December 8...

Take It In The Ear Day. Look it up.

Despite my unabashed affinity for it, I have questions about this holiday. How do I celebrate? What exactly am I supposed to be taking in my ear? And, most importantly, which ear should I take it in?

Perhaps the Christmas season is so long simply because of the lack of ample competition from any other December holiday. Perhaps Christmas helps us forget that Pearl Harbor Day and National Cotton Candy Day fall on the same date, and helps us avoid the inherent bipolar mood swings that this juxtaposition would provoke.

Sure, Christmas is a great holiday, one that billions, young and old, look forward to annually. However, plenty of other holidays encourage family togetherness. Plenty of other holidays encourage wanton spending and lavish consumerism. Furthermore, those individuals, myself included, who point to the birth of Jesus as being a seminal event worthy of extended celebration should be reminded that most scholars agree that Jesus was actually most likely born around September.

This leaves us with two theories as to why we celebrate Christmas in December:

1. The celebration of the birth of Jesus was moved by Pope Julius I in the fourth century A.D. in order to better coincide with the celebration of the Roman winter solstice.

2. Chuck Norris once accidentally sent Jesus a birthday card in December. Jesus was too embarrassed to inform Chuck of his mistake. Thus, we've celebrated Christmas in December ever since.

For the record, I'm not opposed to Christmas claiming the entire month of December. It's kind of a worthless month with nothing else going on. It's the Edsel of months, at least at higher latitudes here in the Northern Hemisphere. And if you're in the Southern Hemisphere, what happens to your Christmas carols this time of year? Do Australian families gather around their air conditioning units and sing "Let It Sun"? Or "Frosty the Foster's"? "Go Tell It In The Outback"? "I Heard The Didgeridoo On Christmas Day"? "Bring A 3-Foot Hunting Knife, Jeanette Isabella"? "Summer Wonderland"? I could go on.

If Yuletide is going to last as long as it does every year, some changes need to take place, especially when it comes to Christmas music. My first suggestion for improvement? Pass laws that prevent this poor excuse for music from being played until, say, around December 23. Anywhere. Everywhere. I mean, "Santa Baby"? Really? How many rich old sugar daddies did the singer confess her love to in exchange for gifts before she settled for one that doesn't actually exist?

And "Come On A My House"? How are you still a free woman, Rosemary Clooney? In the good ol' days, they used to lock people away for confessing to pedophilia, like you do numerous times in this song. Fortunately, you failed to provide your address, so hopefully not too many children were able to take you up on your creepy offer.

My second suggestion would be to update the woefully antiquated ditty "Twelve Days Of Christmas." Not simply in parody form, but by actually permanently altering the original lyrics.

If my true love gave me ten lords a-leaping, I would be taken aback, to say the least, although I'm curious to see how long said lords could maintain their jumping routine. The song implicitly promises me that these lords simply don't quit. If I caught a lord taking a break, could I borrow a drumstick from one of the twelve drummers and beat him with it?

Furthermore, since I don't own cattle, what exactly would those eight maids be milking? Me? And, does anyone even know what a colly bird is? (Yes, that's the original lyric.) It's time to bring this song back to cultural relevance by replacing these hopelessly superannuated gifts with things that members of today's society would actually be happy to receive: divorce papers, welfare checks, and a 40 of Old E.

The last item actually fits neatly into the song, right where the partridge line used to be. Plus, Old E is conveniently sold everywhere. Who knows where you can purchase a pear tree these days, much less a partridge who would be content remaining in one for an extended period of time.

Come to think of it, we might as well overhaul America's entire repertoire of Christmas carols.

"Winter Wonderland" sucks. It must go.

"What Child Is This?" Duh, it's Jesus. Stupid question. Next.

"I Saw Three Ships Come Sailing In"? Good for you, dimbus. You're at a port. Lots of ships sail in daily.

"Carol Of The Bells," "Jingle Bells," "Silver Bells" and "I Heard The Bells On Christmas Day" need an instrument change. Bells are annoying at best. I was forced to play in a bell choir with a bunch of nerdy girls for a few months growing up. This was arguably the worst decision my parents ever made.

And, finally, "Ding Dong Merrily On High"? Stupid. But, if we're going to keep it, let's at least give a nod to other dessert snack makers. Hostess has had the corner on this song, and therefore this market, for far too long.

I would vote for either "Oatmeal Cream Pie Merrily On High," "Star Crunch Merrily On High," or "Zebra Cakes Merrily On High," but I'm open to suggestions.

In reality, we should probably vote in the most austere and revered dessert snack of all, that holiday institution, the gift that keeps on giving. Let's go with "Fruitcake Merrily On High".

Cut. Print. It's a wrap.

ESTA COMIDA LE DA DIARREA.

Can somebody please tell me who holds the job of naming Mexican restaurants?

I want to fight him.

Yeah, I'm convinced that it's just one guy. He's sitting somewhere in a small, sweaty cubicle, running on no sleep, reeking of leftover chimichangas, constantly on his land-line phone with a curly receiver cord, completely out of good ideas.

Let's call him Carlos.

Carlos has, over the years, developed a reputation as THE go-to guy for a quality, authentic-sounding Mexican restaurant name. Considering the business turnover at most of the restaurant buildings near my house, his phone is constantly ringing off the hook.

Carlos is convinced that most Americans don't speak Spanish, and that those who do are too hungry to care that they're eating at a place whose insipid name is translated My House. Or, The New Tijuana. Or, My Hat From Mexico.

Carlos doesn't have much contact with the outside world. If he did, he would know that over 45 million Americans speak Spanish as a first or second language. They see right through his legitimate-sounding restaurant monikers, and realize that the name of their favorite taco house actually means Crazy House Of A Chicken.

There's a restaurant right down the street from where I live called El Jalapenos. No apostrophe, no ñ. Grammatically, this name is a choice representation of the elusive singular/plural quasi-possessive tense.

Fail.

More translated Mexican restaurant names from my neighborhood include My Family, Little House, Big Hat, The Party, Our Kitchen, My Town, May 5, Little Fat Kid, Why Not, Your House, Crazy Burrito, The Cart, Stolen Taco, How Tasty, Happy Duck, The Indian, The Grill, The Pretty House, The Best... need I go on?

My advice is this: if Carlos is operating under the assumption that nobody speaks Spanish, he should get sneaky.

Sneaky like the tattoo artist that inscribes the Chinese character for "stupid American" rather than "peace and prosperity" on the lower back of a sorority girl.

Sneaky like the prominent soy sauce brand that emblazons "No MSG" on its products, yet lists monosodium glutamate in the ingredients.

Carlos, if you think Americans are stupid, then you might as well have a little fun at our expense.

The next Mexican restaurant I get sick from eating at better have a name like Hacemos Nuestra Carne De Gatos. How about Esta Comida Le Da Diarrea? Sus Niños Son Glotones? Estaremos Cerrados En Un Mes?

Su Suegra Es Una Ramera Grande?

Let's at least instill some truth and honesty into this industry.

The movie *Anchorman* had it right. Dinner at Escupimos En Su Alimento, anyone?

LIFE: IT'S WAY TOO SHORT.

I can't stand rush hour.

About the only thing worse than rush hour is thrush hour, that dreaded time of day when young and old alike are temporarily plagued by a whitish parasitic fungus on the insides of their mouths.

The average American spends a total of 38 hours a year stuck in traffic, cursing their lives away. Yesterday afternoon, as I plodded through the last gasps of rush hour traffic on I-84 East in Portland, I popped in a Thrice CD. Yeah, I know. CDs are so 2002. Shut up.

Finally, mercifully, traffic began to clear. I accelerated to almost 50 MPH.

Halfway through "Image Of The Invisible," a semi careened into the fast lane, into the exact spot that my car had been occupying until I slammed on the brakes and veered onto the shoulder. I stopped on the side of the freeway for a minute to hyperventilate, and then cautiously finished my drive home.

My mind was full of thoughts of my own mortality. What if I would've met my end as a mancake on a freeway? What if this were my last day of life? How had I spent my time? Had I made anyone else's life better, or just my own?

Life: it's way too short.

I've already lost six high school and college friends. Three to car or bike accidents; three to suicide. I've been to ten funerals in my life. I tried singing at one of them, but couldn't get through the song without breaking down in tears.

What am I doing with these days and years that I still have?

We get almost eighty years. A couple more if you're lucky. A lot less if you live in Angola.

Crazy to think how much our average life expectancy has increased, and how much our average life accomplishment has shrunk.

When America declared its independence, the average worldwide life expectancy was 35 years. As late as the year 1900, you were expected to live till 47.

Now, we have octogenarians. Nonagenarians. Centenarians. The United States currently has over 70,000 residents who are over 100 years old. When you hit the century mark in this country, you get a letter from the President. Or an open relationship with Newt Gingrich, whichever you prefer.

Newt *is* in his sixties, making him a *sex*agenarian. That's hot.

Sadly, just because we now have more hours of daylight won't stop the sun from setting in the end.

When the sun goes down on each of our lives, will we think back and wish we would've played just one more game of Call Of Duty or put back just one more six-pack? Will we reminisce on all the good times we spent fighting with our significant others, and fondly recall the years spent away from our loved ones working late at the office?

I've occasionally wished that I could foreknow exactly when I will take my last breath. This way, I could at least plan accordingly, and have a pimped-out coffin ready. There are several websites that will count down the seconds remaining in your life for you, assuming you live to an age corresponding with the national average. The truth is, though, that we have no idea when that drunk driver, that heart attack, that stroke, that doctor's error will claim another victim.

I hate death. I hate thinking about it; I hate its capriciousness; I hate all it represents. Yet, it gives meaning to life, its antithesis. If time were unlimited, life would become meaningless.

I'm all in favor of healthy lifestyles; of designated drivers; of medical care. Yet, Americans spend upwards of $50 billion a year on anti-aging products. Some of these dollars go to vanity, to be sure; others are spent in the attempt to slow the hands of time and halt our inevitable march toward the grave.

Of course, I want to live as long as I can. But I'm more concerned with living as *much* as I can. I'll take fifty meaningful, fun-packed, love-filled years over a hundred empty ones in a heartbeat.

I am temporary. However, I am capable of accomplishing something permanent if I use my years wisely.

"We're more than carbon and chemicals; we are the image of the invisible."

So, Death, take me when you will. I'll be ready.

DISCOVER LOVER®.

Nine days till Christmas.

Today, I received four Christmas cards in the mail.

Three were from friends in other states. How thoughtful.

The last card's envelope didn't list a return address, and featured my name, including middle initial, printed in a faux-handwriting font above my address, including my full, +4 ZIP code.

Inside, I found a card covered in adorable little gingerbread men, each one wearing a smile. The card read as follows:

"From our family to yours. Thank you for being a cardmember. We wish you and your family the best during this holiday season. From your friends at Discover®."

This heartwarming message was 'written' in another faux-handwriting font, in red ink, that simulated a seven-year-old's handwriting.

I was deeply moved that someone at Discover® had taken the time to write me a Christmas card. Hurriedly, I canceled all my other credit cards, and went out and purchased lavish gifts, using my Discover® card, and sent them to my friends and family at Discover®. While shopping, I saw a little old lady callously using a

Visa®. So, I sucker-punched her. I must defend the honor of my friends at Discover®, and the honor of their well-deserved interchange fees.

I am a Discover Lover®. They just keep on giving. Why, they even graciously offered me 5% cash back when I shop at Guitarcenter.com, and 20% back at several other online retailers! What a heartwarming Christmas tale. It stands out in stark contrast against the typical profit-first attitudes of most multibillion-dollar corporations. Their ads were right: it pays to Discover®! It pays in smiles, rainbows, gingerbread men, and tears of joy. Oh yeah, and in $48 billion worth of annual interchange fees.

Happy holidays, everyone!

THE KEYBOARD IS MIGHTIER THAN THE NUCLEAR WARHEAD.

If you've made it this far, you might want to know a bit about my life.

If you've made it this far during one sitting on the toilet, you might want to seek medical attention, or at least seek out some prune juice.

If you don't want to know anything about me, too bad. I'm the one holding the pen.

Well, actually, the laptop.

This age of technology has really made numerous old aphorisms obsolete.

"The pen is mightier than the sword" doesn't seem very apropos anymore. Perhaps "the keyboard is mightier than the nuclear warhead" would be more in keeping with the times.

"A picture paints a thousand words" should be updated to "A .jpg Photoshops a thousand Word documents." What it lacks in poetic beauty, it makes up for in product placement for both Adobe and Microsoft. Pay me, corporate America.

This is, indeed, what America is all about. If you succeed, you get rich. If you fail, you write a book about it, the book gets made into a movie, and you get rich.

Obviously, though, money has never been a priority for me; I'm a musician. Next time a homeless person approaches you for a handout, try telling them you play music for a living. They typically do an about-face and offer *you* some change.

I was born in a little town in Michigan. Berrien Center. I'm still not sure what a berrien is, but apparently that's where they all congregate.

I still distinctly remember my fourth birthday and how grown up I thought I was. I also remember getting two boxes of the same crayon set from two different friends and telling them that they were stupid for not having cross-checked their gifts with each other.

When I was almost five, my parents bought a house that sat on 14 acres of woods. This was one of the best decisions they ever made, right behind making love some 9 months before I was born.

Tree houses. Mountain bike trails. Canoeing. Poison ivy, nettles, and 40 hornet stings. I loved those woods.

I'm pretty sure that I was actually more intelligent as a kid than I am now. Actually, IQ tests have confirmed this. I used to read encyclopedias for fun, and memorize impressive-sounding shampoo ingredients.

Methylchloroisothiazolinone. See, I still got it.

I was home schooled for a couple years. During one of these years, my parents took my sister and me to Israel for six months.

My dad, while not remotely Jewy, is a big fan of all things Israel, since he teaches Old Testament and speaks Hebrew. I kind of took being in the Middle East for granted, wondered why the milk was a funny color, and figured that if they changed the name of the Wailing Wall to something more positive, Israelis on the whole would be a lot happier.

I also had the chance to visit Russia, Egypt, Jordan, and about 40 US states before I was ten.

I went to a private elementary and middle school. Oh yeah, and a private high school, too. Played a little football. Wore JNCOs and rocked the extended bowl cut that was shaved up underneath. Don't laugh. Your hair used to look even worse.

I was depressed my sophomore year in high school. Even took some black market Prozac. Turns out that when your closest friends are depressed, chances are you will be too. In addition, I'm pretty sure that it's hard to grow up in Michigan and not be despondent at some point.

Every summer, my family would take a trip to Colorado to see my uncle Bob, and to backpack. I think my dad actually put a backpack on me before I could even walk. He did, however, instill a love of mountains in me. We're still trying to finish up climbing all of the Fourteeners (mountains over 14,000 feet) in Colorado. 44 down, 10 to go.

I was an exchange student in Germany and Austria for six months in 1998. I learned German. I also learned Red Bull and Löwenbräu, and learned that German girls *love* American guys.

I was voted Most Friendly in my senior class. I asked for a second yearbook my senior year because I ran out of room for people to sign in the first one.

They gave me a tacky glue-in insert portion instead. I accidentally managed to adhere it upside-down.

I somehow managed to get a 1600 on the SAT, which has been the only real intellectual achievement of my life to date, much to the chagrin of my parents and sister, who all have their Ph.Ds.

I went to college at Andrews University. Changed my major six times and my hair color probably twenty. Due to my scholarship, I didn't really feel the need to get my money's worth and actually attend class. But, I can't say enough good things about the friends that I made during my five years in undergrad. So, I won't.

I was the frontman for a couple of bands while in college, including The Lemons, with which I got my first taste of touring and my first taste of band drama. Turns out, pregnant keyboardist chicks and rock & roll don't mix.

It wasn't my baby, silly.

Growing up, I had always just planned on going into the field of education; it seemed like the Davidson thing to do. But, on my first day of observation at a 3rd grade classroom my sophomore year, some little punk walked up to me and punched me right in the gonads. This is an absolutely, and painfully, true story.

Since I knew better than to choke him out, I decided to change majors. I finally settled on arguably the most intellectually challenged major of them all, and got my BA in Communications. I dare you to provide me with irrefutable evidence that your major was lamer than mine.

The summer before I graduated, I led worship at a conference for church planters in Chicago. As a result, I got a bunch of job offers.

I visited Portland in June of 2003 to check out one of these potential jobs.

Within the first three days of my trip, I'd gone snowboarding, gone to the beach, jumped off a waterfall, and paid $0 in sales tax.

I'd found my new home.

I was a worship pastor at Mosaic Church in Portland for a year. The pastor got a crush on me. (She was a woman, but it was still weird.) I made some mistakes. I got fired, and the church disintegrated. I could write another three pages about this year, but I've tried to repress these memories, for good reason. I didn't set foot in a church for four years. To this day I'm still not a big fan of organized religion.

I started bartending. What else was I supposed to do with my degree? I guess you could say that my party balls dropped a little late; my 23rd and 24th years went by in a blur.

My boy Tony and I got a great deal on a house in SE Portland. Well, it was a great deal when the housing market was at its peak. I, like millions of other Americans, didn't see the crash coming.

I'm still stuck in this house and contemplating arson.

I started a hard rock/metal band, Silversafe. We had a good run. A couple tours, a single, opening for bands like Puddle Of Mudd, Saliva, Nonpoint, Powerman 5000. I bought a wireless mic and ran a half marathon all over stage during every show.

While in the studio recording with Silversafe, some 'creative differences' (I think this is the PC way to say it) made me decide to record a solo album. I played all the instruments on *Perfect Cliché,* and produced it myself. The album spawned the single “Beautifully Bittersweet”, which spun on 270 stations around the US. Started getting press requests from around the world. I was stoked. I thought my moment had arrived.

It had, but not in the way I’d anticipated.

Probably the greatest thing to come out of this album, the event that meant more to me than any press or accolade, was the girl that came up to me after a show in Coeur d'Alene, ID and told me that the words to the album's title track were what convinced her to forgive her father and call him after 5 years of estrangement.

Still reading? Good. Still sitting on the toilet? Try a prune juice suppository.

Finally, one night in 2008, during a typical battle with insomnia at 4 AM, I lay replaying the events of the day. My uncle Bob had recently died of cancer. A friend from college had just killed herself the day before. I'd gotten in a car accident earlier in the day, and had just had a precancerous growth removed from my shoulder and a benign tumor from my neck.

I couldn't stop thinking about how short life is; how fragile, how precious. It finally hit me that Jesus is in love with me. No ifs, ands or buts. I'd always known this in my head, but never in my heart. It blew up my world. The words "I love you" rang in my ears, as if he'd audibly said them.

During the summer of '09, I went on my third tour as a solo artist. For this one, though, I brought neither band nor merch person; I was truly solo. During a 13-hour drive from Winona, MN to Rapid City, SD in an ice storm, I decided that the socialite in me wasn't cut out for the solo thing. Shortly thereafter, I played a show at Mississippi Studios in Portland with a guy named Russell Stafford.

We dug each other's music, even going so far as developing little musical man-crushes on each other. Just like that, Crown Point was born.

We recorded an EP in Vancouver, BC with Jeff Johnson at Greenhouse Studios. I fell in love with Tim Horton's.

In 2010, we landed the opening slot on the Tyrone Wells and Andrew Belle tour for 35 dates nationwide. I saw firsthand, every night, the genius that is Tyrone Wells sing songs and tell stories that touched on every major category of the human experience: love, God, beauty, pain, longing. Watching, and being a part of, his show for two months straight changed my perspective on what the purpose of music should be.

After another two months on tour in 2011, we began recording our second album. On July 5, though, these plans were put on the back burner when I got into a mountain biking accident, severing my tongue and part of my nose, getting a concussion, and ripping a gash in my lip that required 40 stitches to close. Turns out, it's hard to sing with your mouth in that kind of shape. Who knew?

I am living proof that exercise is bad for you.

In the aftermath of this accident and the hospital bills that ensued, I was simply blown away by the generosity and concern of fans and friends everywhere. Three people I didn't know all that well wrote me sizable checks to help me cover medical bills. A friend of mine who has a bunch of wealthy friends held a fund-raiser for me at his birthday party. And, the body heals. My sense of taste has returned; I can eat solid food; I can sing. I've never been so grateful for things that I would otherwise have taken for granted indefinitely.

I have never been happier to be alive.

I mean that.

Now, it's 2012. I'm busy training for my first marathon, working on my seventh and eighth albums, recovering from our first Australia tour, and writing this, my first book. I'm dealing with rheumatoid arthritis in my left pinkie, which makes both typing and playing guitar rather painful. Amputation is in order.

I have a changed perspective on life, though. Yes, I still have goals to accomplish, but I'm determined not to let my ambitions swallow up my daily life: time spent with the ones I love and with God.

In the words of Switchfoot: "This is your life. Are you who you want to be?"

I'm not who I want to be, not yet. But I'm getting there.

The sheer number of paragraphs that begin with "I" in this chapter is staggering. Come to think of it, this whole book is pretty narcissistic, ad nauseam. Don't like it? Write your own.

LIGHTEN UP.

Obesity sucks.

Ah, that's a weight off my chest.

Pun absolutely intended.

Early-onset disclaimer: I'm not talking about the small percentage of the population who suffer from a thyroid condition or similar ailment that makes avoiding obesity difficult. Having said that, I do know a girl with hypothyroidism who, through hard work, has managed to keep the pounds off. I'm also not talking to those ten- and twenty-pounders among us. Life happens. Our weight fluctuates. No, I'm talking to the people who have to use the electric carts in Safeway for no other reason than the fact that they haven't seen their feet in years. I'm talking fat with a capital F, a capital A, and especially a capital T. Maybe even an extra capital T or two, so the word looks bigger.

Since 63 percent of America is overweight, chances are I've already pissed someone off. But, guess what? Obesity is America's #1 cause of preventable death. America also has the highest percentage of obese people in the world. We are a big, big country.

Go ahead, write me and tell me how I've hurt your feelings, and then go cry into your ice cream.

Yeah, that bowl of Häagen-Dazs Mocha Almond Fudge with 46 grams of fat, 24 grams of saturated fat (120% of your recommended max daily intake), 200 mg of cholesterol, 52 grams of sugar, and 680 calories. In case you're wondering, that's just in one cup. For a full-size container, simply multiply these figures by four.

I'm tired of obesity being too taboo to even discuss. It's America's big little secret.

I'm also tired of it being treated as some collective malady, some capricious killer. Obesity is the result of individual choices by individual people on a daily basis. The blame game ends here.

Why does obesity suck? For starters, it's entirely avoidable. Entirely alterable. Seen "The Biggest Loser"? Ugly people everywhere wish they could be beautiful and get on TV simply by eating right and exercising.

Second, it's rarely genetic. I'd say never, but I'm sure there's some doctor somewhere waiting to pounce on the only fallacy in this book. (All of my other opinions, of course, are sacrosanct fact.) If your idea of family dinner is gorging on KFC and Doritos in front of the TV for the 25th day in a row, your kids will be fat, just like you. If your idea of family exercise is playing Madden with your kids, while gorging on KFC and Doritos, your kids will be fat, just like you.

If, instead, you play real football with your kids, take them hiking and biking, and teach them to eat a balanced diet while consuming fats and sugars in moderation, they will be fit, just like you.

Nurture crushes nature. Literally.

Nurture eats a cheesecake a day, and then plops down awkwardly on nature's chest and suffocates it.

According to a 2010 Gallup survey, obese people are far less likely than people in every other weight category (overweight, normal weight, underweight) to have eaten five servings of fruits and vegetables on at least three days of the past seven.

Third, obesity sucks because we can't call fat people fat. We coin terms like big-boned, ample, and overweight. We open plus-sizes stores. Let's call it what it is. When I'm referred to as white, I don't raise my pinkie (on the hand that's holding my teacup) in warning and insist that people use the word Caucasian, my preferred nomenclature.

Fourth, being fat is not a disability. Have you lost both legs in a land mine explosion while serving our country overseas? *You* have a disability deserving of handicapped tags. When we give morbidly fat people the right to park in handicapped spaces, we're actually ensuring that they have less distance to walk, and ensuring that they will burn as few calories as possible, thus creating a vicious, squishy cycle.

And worst of all, classifying obesity as a disability ensures that some fat people don't have to work (and potentially get exercise in the process), but rather can sit at home in front of their TV on the government's dime, eating Ding Dongs that they've purchased with the food stamps my tax dollars paid for. They can push out a few fat babies to collect some welfare dollars, too.

Fifth, what about travel? I'm not just talking about the fat person in airplane seat 15B who's also oozing across the armrest to take up about 35 percent of your seat 15C. I'm talking about the fact that fat people are partially responsible for higher air fare. According to the Associated Press, obesity leads to airlines spending, in one year alone, almost $300 million extra to pay for the 350 million extra gallons of fuel necessary to transport fat people.[6]

Who pays for this? We do.

You have to pay more if you're carrying extra baggage. Doesn't it stand to reason that you should have to pay more if your body is doing the same thing?

I should also mention the environmental impact. According to the same AP article, fat people cause an average of almost 4 million extra tons of carbon dioxide to be released into the air annually as a result of added weight during air travel. *4 million tons.* Of a gas. This is an unfathomable amount of CO_2, and that figure is not even taking other forms of travel into account.

Sixth, what about the cost to our healthcare system? Universal healthcare would be entirely plausible were it not for obesity. People who are obese are far more likely to report being diagnosed with high blood pressure, high cholesterol, cancer, diabetes, or to have had a heart attack, according to the aforementioned Gallup survey.

Obese people spend 41% more on healthcare and 80% more on prescription drugs annually. Obesity in the US carries the annual price tag of $147 billion in direct medical spending. We spend $147 billion yearly to combat obesity, yet there are still starving children in Africa.

What can be done? I'm not suggesting that we feed fat people to those starving children in Africa. I *am* suggesting that people take responsibility for themselves. Stop blaming a variety of factors for your obesity. If you're fat, chances are you need to exercise more and eat better. That's it. I'm so tired of hearing about fad diets and hypnosis and diet pills. I used to have a fat friend who would constantly complain about how life had dealt him a crappy hand.

He also averaged a Big Mac a day. Coincidence?

Preventative measures are key. Why are kids allowed to drink soda? Ever? What health benefits does it have? Absolutely none.

Plenty of other healthy beverages, such as juice, taste great. How about water? Remember that stuff?

People have no idea what they're eating. Do some research. Just because it has 'salad' in the name doesn't mean it's good for you. Take, for instance, Baja Fresh and its Charbroiled Steak Tostada Salad. Bet you didn't know it has 63 grams of fat (that's more than your recommended daily intake) and more sodium than in 9 orders of McDonald's French fries.

Denny's Double Cheeseburger has 1540 calories and 116 grams of fat. Cold Stone's PB&C shake has 1750 calories, 118 grams of fat (including 64 grams of saturated fat) and 140 grams of sugar. How are these foods even legally sold in America? Where do we draw the line?

Do some research. Don't wallow in your thick ignorance. (Thicknorance?) Nope, diet soda isn't harmless. Sea salt isn't better for you. Taking a multivitamin doesn't make you healthy. Most restaurant food isn't good for you. It's not the potato that makes fries evil. Even light beer has a lot of empty calories. Red meat, especially red meat that's full of preservatives such as carbon monoxide, really has no redeeming health benefits whatsoever.

Why do some parents give in to their child's every culinary whim? Kids' menus at restaurants are disgusting. I dare you to show me a fat kid who is a vegetarian and eats a low-fat, low-refined sugar diet. There are probably two of them on earth, and they are both training hard to become yokozunas.

I've thrown a lot of stats, studies and figures around. Figures on figures, if you will. This book is by no means a scientific treatise. But, by all means, look this stuff up for yourself.

Google is free. And calorie-free.

What are we doing to ourselves? The numbers are staggering. 4 million tons. $147 billion. 63 percent.

It's time to go for a run; time to skip that Big Mac. It's time to shut up and grow up. (I didn't say throw up.)

It's time to lighten up.

THE IMPLICIT AUTHENTICITY OF THE BACK TURD TATTOO.

It must suck being Chris Daughtry's wife.

Worse than being Tiger's. Or Kobe's.

Or Henry VIII's.

Why? Two reasons.

First, they have four kids. Chris is not home much. That's a lot of daily diaper duty.

Second, it seems like most of his big hits are built lyrically on what a waste of a human being she is. He sings "I never saw it coming, I should've started running a long, long time ago" to thousands of people every night, and then calls home and tells her how much he loves her.

Let's not forget "You Don't Belong," "No Surprise," "Life After You," and "I Kicked You To The Curb And Then Tattooed A Turd On Your Back While You Were Drunk, You Cheating Hooker." The latter song will be on Daughtry's upcoming Internet-phenomenon-based country album, I'm told.

This, boys and girls, is known as the art of selling out. Fans relate to Daughtry's insincere attempt at feigning heartache, even though a simple Wikipedia search will tell you that he and his wife are still together. Everyone wants to believe that somebody's life sucks worse than theirs.

I could write and perform a shoddy mini-opera about how much some of Daughtry's lyrics bore me. How many times has this guy really been stepped on by cruel women throughout the course of his marriage?

I will say, though, that if the man's voice were a beautiful woman, I would probably think naughty thoughts about it. Also, Chris has done incredible amounts of philanthropic work, both in and out of the spotlight.

So, what's the point? I suppose that the fault lies with me and my inability to throw aside my subconscious demands for authenticity and substance in music. I am not too school for cool. Just get dancy.

Why so serious?

It's hard to raise my glass and type with both hands simultaneously, but I'm trying. This book is not going to write itself!

Why do I even bother to listen to lyrics, anyway? Recently, I was driving to Bend, OR with a friend when "Marry You" by Bruno Mars came on. My friend gushed about what a sweet, romantic man Bruno must be for having written such a touching love song. He'd heard enough of the lyrics to realize the song was about marriage, but not enough to realize that Bruno was talking about a Vegas wedding, complete with shots of Patrón and the distinct possibility of annulment the next day.

By the way, Bruno's given name is Peter Gene Hernandez. How authentic of him. But, realistically, I probably would've gone with

Bruno, too, in homage to Sacha Baron Cohen's touching film about love from an intercultural perspective.

Speaking of authenticity, and touching on a previous point, I desperately want to believe that the trending picture of some Ohio girl's back-turd tattoo is real. In this digital, Photoshopped age, I'm clinging to this picture's implicit authenticity. I need an anchor, and I've found it here in this unfortunate, permanent back poop art.

And, just so you stop wallowing in your ignorance, Pink's real name is Alecia Moore, and Daughtry's is, well, Christopher Daughtry.

Yup, more fun-filled facts to know and share.

If Ke$ha is the reinvention of pop music, as she claims, then the fate of lyrics in general has officially been sealed. Case closed.

So, from now on, I resolve to shun lyrics altogether. I wouldn't feel right about writing the throwaway lyrics about sex, partying, and breakups that everyone wants to hear, so I'm doing away with them entirely.

Look for Crown Point's new album to exclusively feature unintelligible yelps, grunts and gestures (the latter of which you might not be able to hear).

Think David Lee Roth meets Helen Keller.

You're welcome.

ALL OF OUR PRECIOUS SHEEP.

Ever hear of the boy who cried wolf?

Too bad old Aesop was behind on the times. He didn't even reference the obvious parallels to social media *once* in this fable.

Thankfully, I'm here to bring Aesop up to date.

Everybody is crying wolf. Every day. On Facebook.

I just read and categorized the last one hundred posts by my 'friends' on my personal Facebook page.

This is cold, hard science cominatcha. Here they are, with posts broken down by category, in no particular order:

You just watched the best movie ever: 6 posts.

You just made dinner, probably in the microwave, and had to let people know what you ate and why you had to take an agonizing 20-minute leave of absence from Facebook: 7 posts.

Your clumsy kid got a boo-boo: 4 posts.

You're flying somewhere boring and cold in the morning: 6 posts.

You watched tonight's college football game and apparently know more than both coaches: 10 posts.

You went to the gym to try some fad workout: 4 posts.

Your social life consists of watching TV shows: 6 posts.

You posted something cryptic that even you don't understand: 4 posts.

You thought some stale aphorism is deeply life-changing, and were compelled to share it: 2 posts.

You shamelessly promoted yourself: 18 posts.

You thought your kids were cute: 3 posts.

You posted a picture of your kids that even you couldn't possibly think was cute: 5 posts.

You got all your political views from a YouTube video, and had to share the link: 2 posts.

You took and shared a picture of yourself doing something mind-numbingly stupid: 5 posts.

You complained about something trivial, like a headache or a long line at the grocery store, while millions die of hunger: 13 posts.

You just wasted part of your life watching a stupid video, and the only way to make yourself feel better about it is to trick other people into wasting their lives by watching it too: 4 posts.

Okay, so you fact-checked me by doing the math. I actually read the last ninety-nine posts. Glad to see you're paying attention.

99 posts of poop on the wall. Put *that* in a children's song. At least it won't be as creepy as "Rub-A-Dub-Dub, Three Men In A Tub."

These 99 posts are a cross-section of what I think represents a pretty typical Facebook stream.

A stream replete with a constant barrage of complaints, half-wit humor, and self-aggrandizing PR.

Google+ users, don't think you're any better. Neither are all three of you still using MySpace.

You, like most Americans, have spent the last few years crowding cyberspace by pumping out mindless drivel about what you're eating and how much your hangnail hurts, and now you have something important to say. Maybe you're getting married. Maybe you're getting syphilis. Maybe you're getting both. Unfortunately, you've been blocked or de-friended or just generally tuned out, and you just got a grand total of 3 'likes' and one blasé comment on your earth-shattering Facebook post.

I'm not saying that I'm the most interesting Facebooker I know. The only reason I'm not saying it is because it would sound conceited.

The fact that I could care less about the meaningless new workout you just tried or the crappy new TV show that just changed your life means that I should reasonably assume that you don't care about the menial contents of my day's agenda, either.

Maybe you *do* care. This is an even scarier thought. Really? You have nothing better to think about than what *I'm* reading while on the toilet? (If you must know, it's this book, of course.)

I know that we all want to have what we say matter, even in the doldrums of our everyday existence. But that's what your close friends, your spouse, your boyfriend, or your parents are for.

Tell them that your little Jimmy has an owwie and you gave him a Mickey Mouse Band-Aid. Don't tell me. I could care less. Unless, of course, you were all out of Mickey and were forced to administer the Minnie Mouse version, which made poor emasculated Jimmy bawl.

That would at least entertain me. Am I a terrible person? Actually, don't answer that.

My point is this: If your post doesn't make me laugh, or make me think, or make me a little more knowledgeable, I don't want it in my eyeballs.

You're probably wondering why I'm even on Facebook at all. Truth is, I've already lost all hope in humanity's ability to rein in the constant stream of verbal sewage spewing out of its collective mouth. So, I almost never check Facebook's activity stream, or its timeline. Or its anything. If I want to see what you've been up to, I will call you or email you. We might even set up a time to hang out. In person. Like human beings.

I will admit that there are a few people in my Facebook life whose pages I regularly go to so as to suckle from the teat of wisdom that they possess. These people get it. They understand that life is not about quantity; it's about quality. It's not just about making as much noise as you can, but rather about making beautiful metaphorical music.

I will also admit that I'm a hypocrite. I, too, have been guilty on plenty of occasions of several of the seven deadly Facebook sins. I self-promote. I discuss my day's mundane activities. I make much ado about nothing sometimes. And yes, my cat Minisaurus has her own Facebook page.

Yes, I complain a lot on Facebook. Sometimes facetiously; sometimes not. I have no plans to buck that trend in the near future.

I also have no plans to doe or fawn said trend. I just wanted you to know that I know that you know.

But hey, it's much easier for me to sit here and judge you than it is to judge myself. So, shut up and take it like a man, or whatever it is that you are.

I simply wish that Facebook would have turned out differently. If everyone, myself included, posted half as many times a day and made each post twice as compelling, intriguing, engaging, or entertaining, would I feel better about social media, and ultimately, about society in general? You bet.

We need to filter our thoughts. Keep those 99 poopy posts to ourselves. Make our words count. Otherwise, no one will be there to help us fend off the wolf as it devours all of our precious sheep.

REVENGE OF THE GOOEY BROWN DEMON.

My worst day on a mountain didn't involve a broken limb, an ice storm, or a bivouac.

Or a cougar. Cougars generally look for their prey in bars these days, anyway.

My worst day on a mountain was far worse. It took place on Little Bear Peak, in the heart of Colorado's Sangre de Cristo Mountains.

I've been climbing mountains since I was a fetus. I've climbed eight of the Cascade volcanoes, 44 of the 54 mountains over 14,000 feet in Colorado, three Fourteeners in California, and 26 of the 50 highest points in each US state. Yes, I'm bragging. I've encountered lightning storms on the summits of Mt. Wilson and Kit Carson Peak, and 100-mph winds on Mt. Hood and Mt. Washington. I've had to bivouac in the freezing cold with nothing but an emergency blanket on Mt. Whitney and Dog Mountain. I've been in quite a few situations where one misstep on a ledge or one bad move on a rock face would send me hurtling to my death.

However, none of it holds a candle to the misfortune I suffered on Little Bear.

To give you a little background, there is nothing little about Little Bear. Rising to 14,037 feet, it has the reputation of being one of the hardest Fourteeners to climb in Colorado. The route features a 300′ water-polished Class 4/low class 5 pitch known as the Hourglass, due to the fact that all rockfall from the chutes above funnels directly into it. It has claimed the lives of at least 8 climbers in the past 50 years.

My dad, my sister's ex-husband (who, turns out, is a psychopath), and I had backpacked into Lake Como to climb Little Bear and a couple of adjacent peaks. After four days of nothing but backpacking 'food', my GI tract was more than a little upset with me. I'm used to that, though, so we pressed on with our final objective: Little Bear.

We left around 5 AM, summiting close to 11. We took the requisite summit shots, climbing helmets still on, and my dad relieved himself on top. We headed back down in somewhat of a hurry, hoping that the afternoon thunderstorms wouldn't find us still downclimbing Little Bear's technical pitches.

After traversing the mountain's notoriously exposed knife-edge ridge, climbing down a rotten class 4 chute, and rappelling down the Hourglass, it hit me.

Explosive, uncontrollable diarrhea.[7]

Perched on a ledge with a 1500-foot cliff below me, I let nature run its impetuous course. Forget Angry Birds. I had Angry Turds.

TMI? Of course. I almost omitted this chapter. You're welcome.

Wealthy members of ancient Roman society used to use imported Portuguese urine as mouthwash. See? Other people are gross, too.

It hit me that I had failed to bring any toilet paper along. I yelled up to my dad to bring me some. This is how families grow closer together. With horror, my usually responsible father realized he had left his roll on top of Little Bear.

With a thousand vertical feet of cliffs and loose rock between us and the summit, and with thunderstorms rolling in, I had no choice but to improvise.

First to go was a Clif Bar wrapper. Then, I turned to an ACE Bandage, a sock, and some thorny foliage.

Without going into too much detail, there was a lot of work to be done in the wiping department.

A few minutes later, the gooey brown demon inside me reared his ugly head again. I'd never experienced anything quite like this. Having decided quickly that the thorny foliage was a very bad idea, I dug around for the smoothest-looking rocks I could find on the little ledge I had made my throne.

After repeating this grisly, repugnant scenario several more times, we descended back to the Lake Como valley, where a stream mercifully awaited. Mother Nature's bidet, just for me. 38-degree glacier water had never felt so good.

Dad actually took some pictures of me in the throes of anguish, holding a rock in one hand. As a public service, and to avoid the "Parental Advisory" insignia on the cover, I have decided not to print any of them in this book. Apologies.

I've now begun popping an Imodium at the start of each climb. It's worked scatological wonders, except for on a backpacking trip in Tennessee. Somehow, I overdosed and didn't go for a week.

But, I'll save that for Volume Number 2. Ha. I just said 'Number 2.'

RICKY MARTIN AND A PARTRIDGE IN A PEAR TREE.

Ricky Martin made headlines some months ago, for the first time in a while.

He formally announced that he is gay.

In other news, the Pope has finally come out and revealed that he is Catholic, and Ron Jeremy is expected to declare that he is of above average endowment later this week.

It's about time, Ricky. You had us all fooled. Or perhaps there is something we don't know about Rebecca De Alba's anatomy.

How was this news? It's as if the Chicago Tribune had decided to run an exposé on the fact that the Cubs do, in fact, suck.

I will admit: I still took the time to read the story. On two different websites.

It's mind-boggling to think of how much time I spend on menial activities, like reading said quasi-news stories, or folding my underwear, or attempting to get the ends of a trash bag open so I can line a trash can with it. I estimate that I spend at least 30 profanity-laden seconds per trash-bag change, which happens probably twice a week. That's a minute a week, wasted. Gone. 52

minutes a year. If I live to be 85, I will have spent 73.6 hours, or just over three full days of my life, wrestling with my plastic nemeses.

I wish I could just get all three of those days out of the way at once. Maybe. That *is* a lot of sack to deal with in a short period of time. Perhaps Ricky Martin would be willing to help out.

I slept in today. Got to bed at 1:30, and woke up at 10:45. I honestly cannot recall the last time I had a chance to do that. I can't comprehend the fact that the average American watches six hours of TV a day. Six hours? Since canceling my cable last year, I haven't even watched a total of six hours of TV since. It seems silly to live through imaginary people's lives when you could be living your own.

And don't even get me started on those social media games. From the comfort of your own profile, you can start a food fight. You can join the mafia. You can buy your friends as pets. You can buy a partridge in a pear tree. You can get poked, groped and fondled. You can even get pooped on. Look it up.

I really don't get it. Is there really nothing better you could be doing with your life? Even Solitaire requires some sort of mental function. Sadly, this inanity is indicative of society at large, and not just of some lunatic fringe. What could possibly be so important that it would keep the typical American from hitting the gym, writing their grandparents, getting an education, being a contributing family member, and pursuing a lasting and rewarding career? SuperPets, that's what. One hundred years ago, kids worked on the farm. Now, they work on Farmville.

In the thirty minutes that I've spent writing today, I've gotten requests on Facebook to join CastleVille, Ravenskye City, and Sims Social, and have been gifted a zebra, which I am supposed to send back. Let me spell it out for you: If anybody sends me a zebra, or any other large, multicolored ungulate, I'm keeping it. No ifs, ands, or bison, okapi? You'd be lucky if I even returned a wallaby. Most likely, it would be AWOLaby.

While no one would accuse me of lacking an opinion on the matter, I'm not saying free time is a bad thing. A total lack of it is enough to drive anyone crazy.

I firmly believe that there is no such thing as luck, whether you're a musician, an entrepreneur, a plumber, a gigolo. The harder you work to put yourself in the right place, the more likely you are to experience what outsiders might categorize as good luck.

There is also no such thing as time wasted. With every minute of your life, you make a decision. You decide how to spend it. We are all getting older, together; the hourglass of time is a relentless foe. It's an endless march of sand, as Thrice puts it. How we spend our time determines who we are becoming.

If your time is spent on yourself, you will end up a selfish person. If your time is spent giving, you will end up a loving individual. If your time is spent rooting for the Seattle Seahawks, you will probably wish you were dead.

It's no easy road, spending time on things that matter. Why not put off for tomorrow what we should be doing today?

In the words of the title track of my last solo album, "Perfect Cliché:" "Difficult to try and quell the insurrection of time against the soul. And now you're left with the regret of all that's left undone and unsaid, but who collects on emotional debts anyway? Maybe today, and maybe tomorrow; maybe before your time is taken away. Maybe today you'll break what you've borrowed, or maybe you'll mend it with a perfect cliché."

Time is precious. Spend it wisely.

THANKFUL.

I've spent a lot of time with myself over the years (practically every waking second), and I've come to realize, much to my chagrin, that I don't say thanks enough.

So, it's time. It's Thanks O'Clock.

At the beginning of this book, I promised that I would say thanks to you if you made it this far.

So, thanks. To you. Thanks for reading this book. Thanks for buying CDs, for coming to a show, for taking the time to write and let me know that one of our songs means something to you. Thanks even for downloading my music illegally and sharing it with a friend. Or a sworn enemy.

Don't get a big head, though. I'm thankful for more than just you.

Come to think of it, I'm thankful for a lot.

I'm thankful for Multi-Grain Cheerios and barbecue sauce.

I'm thankful for cats. For dogs. For wombats. I've never actually had the opportunity to be thankful for a specific wombat, but I'm thankful for them in general. They are unbelievably cute.

I'm thankful for coffee. For tea. For energy drinks. Basically, for caffeine itself.

I'm thankful for waterfalls. Thankful for mountains and for the legs to climb them. Thankful for the lavish beauty that surrounds me here in Oregon.

I'm thankful for mirrors. Not only because they enable me to remind myself of how good I look, but also because they enable me to go out in public sans spinach in my teeth. Or Dots. I still have a red one stuck in my molar from last week.

I'm thankful for running water. For hand sanitizer. For a country free, for the most part, of bubonic plague.

I'm thankful that life is a blank page. Thankful that we are capable of change, capable of love, capable of forgiveness.

I'm thankful for jungle gyms and trampolines.

I'm thankful for Thrice. For Live. For Needtobreathe. For AWOLNATION. For a thousand other bands and artists. For music.

I'm thankful for friends. For those rare, genuine people in your life who will tell it like it is. I'm thankful for brutal honesty.

I'm thankful for freeways. For crampons. For binoculars. For smart phones. For Catch Phrase. For Shazam. For digital photography. For Wikipedia. For bar codes. For the Camelbak. For skydiving. For Advil. For all the good that man hath wrought.

I'm thankful for public restrooms. For periodicals. For freedom of speech.

I'm thankful for Mandy. Even though things didn't work out, you still taught me more in four years than I've learned from any other human being in my lifetime.

I'm thankful, in a weird sort of way, for pain and hardship. I never seem to get my priorities straight when the going is easy.

I'm thankful for a God who loves me more than his own life.

I'm thankful for happiness. For sadness. For the range of emotions that we as humans experience, each one with the capability to put another in perspective.

I'm thankful that a day is coming when our question marks will be turned into exclamation points.

I'm thankful for today. For this hour. For this minute.

I'm thankful that I'm alive.

AFTERWORD.

You have reached the end of this book.

You probably picked up on that fact without me having to point it out to you.

Hopefully, you've enjoyed it. If not, I encourage you to please recycle this volume, or to regift it to your creepy uncle Willy.

Also, keep in mind that I am in no way liable if you are arrested for mentioning the name of this book in an airport or on an airplane.

Sayōnara.

NOTES.

1. Michael Pollan, *The Botany Of Desire: A Plant's-Eye View Of The World* (New York: Random House, 2002), 201.
2. I can't believe you actually looked up this endnote. You're an idiot.
3. Rictor Norton, "Reflections on Gay History," *Gay History and Literature,* http://rictornorton.co.uk/history.htm (June 4, 2007).
4. C. David Coats, *Old MacDonald's Factory Farm: The Myth Of The Traditional Farm And The Shocking Truth About Animal Suffering In Today's Agribusiness* (New York: Continuum Int'l Publishing Group, 1989), Preface.
5. Mark Gotti, *Jesus Mean And Wild: The Unexpected Love Of An Untamable God* (Grand Rapids: Baker, 2008), 171.
6. Associated Press, "Feds: Obesity Raising Airline Fuel Costs," http://www.usatoday.com/travel/news/2004-11-05-obese-fliers_x.htm (November 5, 2004).
7. Why would you possibly want to know more about this? You disgust me. See Endnote 2.

ABOUT THE AUTHOR.

Jon Davidson is some guy who lives in Portland, OR. This is his first book. He has released six studio albums with several bands and produced albums for four artists. Jon has written a lot of songs, some of which suck. The ones that don't ended up on albums, and have been played on over 275 radio stations across the US and Canada.

Jon writes left-handed, plays guitar right-handed, loves coffee, enjoys mountain biking, can and will crush you at Boggle, and is fond of run-on sentences. Jon has climbed over 100 mountains, including 47 over 14,000 feet. In addition to playing music, Jon has worked as a bartender, a worship pastor, a clothing store manager, a booker for a music venue, a groundskeeper, a computer consultant, and a call center phone operator. He has never worked as a fluffer at any time.

Jon has a BA in Communications from Andrews University in Berrien Springs, MI, and has served on the editorial staff of three newspapers. He is currently the frontman for the band Crown Point, and is somewhat obsessed with his unbelievably adorable cat, Minisaurus. Jon writes a blog, Rhetorock, which can be found at jondavidsonmusic.blogspot.com, or at his official website, jondavidsonmusic.com.

You can contact, laud, compliment, praise, extol, and commend Jon by email at jon@jondavidsonmusic.com. All negative feedback can be directed to yourlifesucks@notarealemailaddress.com.

www.ingramcontent.com/pod-product-compliance
Lightning Source LLC
Chambersburg PA
CBHW060249050426
42448CB00009B/1599

* 9 7 8 0 6 1 5 6 0 1 1 0 6 *